CAUGHT IN
THE ACT

Eye witness: Melody MacDonald joins Professor Feldberg in his laboratory.

CAUGHT IN THE ACT
The Feldberg Investigation

Melody MacDonald
and the
Animal Cruelty
Investigation Group

Foreword by
Dr Michael Fox

Compiled and edited by
Jill Russell

JON CARPENTER
Oxford

First published in 1994 by
Jon Carpenter Publishing
PO Box 129, Oxford OX1 4PH

The right of Melody MacDonald and other named contributors to be
identified as the authors of this work is hereby asserted in accordance with the
Copyright, Designs and Patents Act 1988.

The photographs on pages (ii), 17, 22, 34, 36, 50, and 54 are the copyright of
Advocates for Animals and the Animal Cruelty Investigation Group. The
photograph on page 29 is the copyright of Dr Michael W. Fox. The cartoon on
page (i) is reproduced by kind permission of Colin Wheeler. The title *Caught in
the Act* is courtesy of Tim Phillips of *Turning Point* magazine.

ISBN 1 897766 05 X

Designed and typeset by Sarah Tyzack, Oxford.
Printed and bound by Biddles Ltd, Guildford, England.

Contents

*These chapters include material from video and audio tapes recorded by Mike Huskisson, copyright Advocates for Animals, 10 Queensferry Street, Edinburgh EH2 4PG and the Animal Cruelty Investigation Group, PO Box 8, Halesworth, Suffolk IP 19 0JL.

DEDICATION

This book is dedicated to the millions of animals who suffer and die every day in research laboratories all over the world. May they rest for ever in love, comfort and peace.

'The idea, as I understand it, is that fundamental truths are revealed in laboratory experimentation on lower animals and are then applied to the problems of the sick patient. Having been myself trained as a physiologist, I feel in a way competent to assess such a claim. It is plain nonsense.'

SIR GEORGE PICKERING,
Regius Professor of Medicine at the University of Oxford,
British Medical Journal, Dec 26 1964.

'...the animals...are the victims of mankind's habit of subordinating all creatures to his own purposes.'

LORD JUSTICE LESLIE SCARMAN,
Personal Communication to R. MacDonald, 1989.

'The divine right of scientists to operate above the law and the imperialistic attitude of the biomedical establishment to outside censure are hallmarks of a rising technocracy that are anathema to a truly civilised society.'

DR MICHAEL W. FOX, MRCVS, 1990

'Indeed it has been said that if all laboratory and scientific research were halted for a few years and strenuous efforts were made to implement confirmed public health measures then enormous good would result.'

ARTHUR C. KENNEDY, FRCP,
Presidential Address to the British Medical Association, 1991.

'We have helped both in the enforcement of the law and the upgrading of it. We will continue to do so until our fellow creatures are treated with the respect that is their birthright.'

MIKE HUSKISSON, January 1992.

Acknowledgements

I COULD NEVER have achieved what I set out to do without the invaluable help and support of several people. My special thanks go to my great friend and mentor *Jill Russell*, who originally alerted me to Professor Feldberg's research, never gave up, undertook extensive background research for this book, and gave me much needed encouragement and moral support; to Jill's family and friends; *Mike Huskisson*, who was responsible for filming the vital video recorded evidence which we so badly needed, also thanks for permission to use his photographic, audio and video-taped evidence; *my mother*, who was a tower of moral strength and inspiration; my good friend *Dr Michael Fox*, who braved the laboratory with me, gave me guidance and professional veterinary advice, and for kind permission to use his photographs; *Lorraine Richter*, for her bravery and support in joining me on that first day in the laboratory when I was feeling so nervous; *Bill Jordan*, who advised Mike Huskisson and myself on the veterinary angle of the situation in the laboratory; *Les Ward* and *Advocates for Animals*, for giving the whole episode much needed publicity and financial backing, and for advice and permission to use their transcripts, reports, video-tapes and photographs; the editor of *New Scientist* for permission to quote from a recent article on scientists' views on animal experiments; *Dr Vernon Coleman*, a stalwart anti-vivisection campaigner and medical doctor; *Matthew Hall*, Barrister, and *Sir David Napley*, who gave me their time and expert legal advice; *Gareth Jones* at World in Action for advice on copyright; *Helen Henzel*, a former laboratory technician for professional advice; *Eve Hodson* for encouragement and dedicated help; and many medical doctors, good friends and fellow kindred spirits who were so supportive to me in this quest for justice for the Animal Kingdom; and finally to my dear friend *Virginia McKenna* who has been a wonderful example to me of sheer determination combined with beauty and dedication for our poor suffering friends 'The Animals'.

Melody MacDonald, 1993.

Preface

I REMEMBER IN 1987 speaking to my friend Lord Selkirk who, with his wife, is a great supporter of animal rights. He told me that his mother, the late Duchess of Hamilton, had campaigned all her life for justice for the animal kingdom and that, like her, I had a long road ahead of me if I was to achieve any goals. I told him I saw a great similarity between slavery and vivisection and asked him how he thought one could best abolish it, as William Wilberforce had indeed managed to abolish slavery in 1807. His words of advice, as I remember them, were for the subject to be aired openly in society in drawing rooms across the land, not secretly in back rooms or behind closed doors. This apparently was how changes were effected and hence slavery ended. This exposé has certainly helped to bring the subject of animal experimentation to public attention and, as we will see, even scientists are now discussing the matter openly.

I feel strongly that one day people *will* look back in horror at vivisection and realise that apart from being totally unscientific, cruel and barbaric, it is also an archaic practice. Modern scientific methods of research will replace it and the pharmaceutical and agrochemical giants will no longer be able to manipulate the unsuspecting public, creating vast profits out of animal suffering and calculated cruelty with the phoney alibi of 'saving human lives and curing the sick.' Along with zoos and circuses it will very soon, we hope, be a relic of the past but until that day the crusade will continue.

Melody MacDonald, 1993.

Foreword

Dr Michael W. Fox, DSc, PhD, BVetMed, MRCVS,
Vice-President, The Humane Society of the United States

THROUGH MY INVOLVEMENT in the Feldberg exposé (which was really an exposé of the British biomedical establishment) I came to appreciate two kinds of single-mindedness. What distinguished the one from the other was a matter of compassion. Without the compassionate single-mindedness of Melody MacDonald, the scientific priesthood would have remained immune from public censure. Yet she entered the hallowed halls of the Medical Research Council (MRC), and with great courage sat through one experiment after another, observing Professor Feldberg and his research assistant working on cat after cat and rabbit after rabbit.

I had known Melody for about one year before she started her investigation. Knowing what an empathic soul she is, I was deeply concerned for her own well-being, having to witness Feldberg at his vivisection table time after time as she gained his confidence and built up her case against him. Her courage and perseverance saw her through. While she had single-mindedly and single-handedly gained access to the MRC, she knew that without other potential witnesses—expert witnesses if possible—plus photographic and video documentation of Feldberg's experiments, her efforts and anguish would amount to naught.

So she asked me if I might go with her to see Feldberg the next time I came over from America. She gave me several of Feldberg's scientific papers to read prior to my visit, and as we approached the MRC laboratory, I had a vivid flash-back of my past life as a research scientist. It was indeed a life-time past, since my attitude towards animals, and how I valued the knowledge derived from

1

vivisection, had changed radically. As a research scientist, I valued the 'objectivity' of the scientific method, the excitement of making new discoveries and the ego-gratification of having one's findings published. I put myself into this now alien mind-set, as I signed the MRC visitor's book and clipped my visitor's tag to my blazer lapel in preparation for my day with Feldberg in his laboratory.

After half an hour talking with 'the Prof' (as he was respectfully addressed by his assistant and associates), I realised that I was conversing with a single-minded scientist with a consuming passion for research. Soon, his assistant had a cat ready for the day's experiment. Feldberg was showing his age and kept forgetting when he had taken the last blood sample, which he insisted on trying to draw himself in spite of the tremor in his hands. I vacillated between feeling sympathy and pity for him and for the cat, but as the experiment progressed, my sense of outrage intensified. In my opinion, the experiment was pointless, the technique crude, and the data appeared to be collected according to no set protocol nor with any scientifically valid or testable hypothesis.

It was difficult to contain my outrage when the anaesthetised cat, on an artificial respirator, was left unattended while we were both invited to take a tea break with other colleagues in the canteen. The tea break chit-chat was as meaningless as the experiment, I thought. I hoped, for the cat's sake, that it would be dead when we returned half an hour later. But the cat was still alive.

The Prof took another temperature reading and blood sample from the cat, switched off the respirator and started to dissect it alive. He was looking to find certain nerves in the cat's abdominal cavity to check that he had correctly severed them earlier in the day as part of the experiment. I saw that they were still intact and he was annoyed that the day had been wasted—as well as the cat, which he said had cost well over £100. He then cut open the cat's chest cavity, pulled out its beating heart and then cut the heart out, placing it on top of the cat's chest. The experiment was finished by such a bizarre ritual that I was in complete shock.

The words of his assistant, 'Oh, you're doing a live dissection today, Prof,' were still ringing in my ears as Melody and I drove him home, on his insistence, to have a drink and chat for a while. Needless to say, the conversation was entirely one-sided, Feldberg revealing even more of his total self-involvement and complete lack of interest in anything or anyone beyond his own single-minded obsession with the 'research' he was conducting on the regulation of blood sugar levels. This particular line of research was initiated after he found that the blood sugar level was elevated in one of his experimental animals after a reading lamp placed over the animal had fallen onto the animal's abdomen and burned it while they left it unattended during a tea-break.

This entire experience confirmed Melody's impression that Feldberg was no longer competent to experiment on animals and that he was held in such high regard by his peers that no-one dared question either his competence or the scientific validity and medical relevance of his work. As an FRS and Professor Emeritus with a host of honorary degrees and other honours, he was beyond reproach. Yet the scientific priesthood was as much to blame as he, for in continuing to fund his research, they facilitated his downfall, lost their own credibility in the public's eye, and allowed a greater tragedy—the needless suffering of experimental animals. Without the continued dedication of people like Melody MacDonald and Mike Huskisson, such suffering will continue in the name of scientific knowledge and medical progress. But humanity will not be the better for it, since no good ends can come from evil means.

Introduction

In the Beginning...
Jill Russell

ON SUNDAY, 6 MAY 1990, at 4 pm, I received a telephone call which I will never forget. Melody sounded very cool but obviously triumphant. She told me that her long and harrowing investigation into Professor Wilhelm Feldberg's research had finally resulted in his licence to experiment on animals being revoked by the Home Office on the previous Friday.

Certainly I never imagined such a thing could or would ever happen when, in 1984, I read a letter in the local press which introduced me to the nightmare world of vivisection. It described smoking and alcohol experiments on animals which I found hard to believe. I began reading scientific journals to see for myself what was going on in animal research laboratories.

I was appalled by what I read. I had heard that only the 'top' 20 per cent of research was ever published. I could not even imagine what the rejected research must have been like.

I contacted the writer of the letter who arranged for me to meet Fay Fullerton, another doctor's wife. She was a very compassionate local animal welfarist and invited me to visit her. She was very kind and helpful and over coffee gave me books and antivivisection leaflets; a mere glance at the illustrations made me determined to try to help these poor animals.

As I drove along the lovely country lane from her woodland home I could not help but contrast the freedom of the wild animals I saw with the conditions which I now knew laboratory animals had to endure.

Until that time, I had never given much thought to animal

research. I had always thought of biomedical research as being very high-tech with brilliant scientists in space-age laboratories making incredible discoveries—a scenario I now realise we are all supposed to believe.

I very quickly discarded that illusion when I saw a video recording of the notorious Pennsylvania primates head injury research which had links with Glasgow University.[1] It was absolutely shocking. The research was subsequently stopped but tragically has been started again recently using different species. However, that video made me quite determined to find out the truth of what else was going on in the name of medical research.

Some of the cruellest animal experiments come under the heading of 'basic research'—that is to say, they are not performed to investigate a particular problem. The reason for performing such experiments is frequently not stated in scientific reports, and they appear to be undertaken because they just might throw some light on something, someday. In other words, the main motive is curiosity.

Amongst the published British experiments which most horrified me were those undertaken by W.S. Feldberg. I first came across his name when I read about conscious cat brain experiments which had taken place in London in the 1950s.[2] They sounded barbaric (excerpts from Feldberg's own descriptions of his early experiments are included later in this chapter) but I assumed they would have stopped long ago; however, they made such an impression on me that I clearly remembered the scientist's name.

It was quite by chance, and with some surprise, that I came across his research again when, in 1985, I happened to read a medical journal which contained an article by Feldberg and his colleagues.[3] It stated that Claude Bernard (a nineteenth-century French physiologist renowned for his exceptionally callous and cruel experiments on conscious animals) had discovered nearly a hundred and fifty years previously that injuring part of a rabbit's brain caused a rise in the rabbit's blood sugar levels.

Feldberg had extended these experiments to include the effects of drugs. He gave many references to his own research which mentioned the use of cats: The experiments were similar to those I had read about before and were obviously still going on thirty years later, so I decided to investigate his work more extensively.

A friend looked him up in *Who's Who*. Under Recreations he listed 'women's fashions'. At the time we had no idea how useful this innocent piece of information was to be...

From *Who's Who* I also discovered that he had been born in 1900. I had not known his age previously but it was extraordinary that a man of this age, almost a quarter of a century older than the compulsory retirement age for NHS surgeons, should be allowed to continue to operate on animals.

Feldberg had started experimenting early. At the age of five he had tried to breathe life into a clay model of a doll he had made.[4] This being unsuccessful he had later proceeded to take life away from countless innocent animals for over sixty years.

Working at the National Institute for Medical Research (NIMR) at Mill Hill, London, Feldberg was using conscious cats. First they were starved for several hours; then, under anaesthetic, they had holes drilled in their skulls. Cannulae (thin tubes) were inserted through the holes into the ventricles (fluid-filled cavities) of their brains and cemented in place. The cats were then allowed to 'recover' for about three days and then were starved yet again for at least eighteen hours before the experiment started.

The experiments consisted of the injection of noxious substances such as strychnine, curare, anti-freeze and LSD through the cannulae directly into the ventricles of the conscious cats' brains. The cats were then observed to see what happened.

From Feldberg's own published descriptions the cats suffered horrible effects including vomiting, catalepsy, pilo-erection (i.e. hair standing on end), fits, shivering, growling, yelping, incontinence, involuntary scratching movements, panting, salivation, meowing and so-called 'sham rage.' Detailed descriptions are provided in the following examples from Feldberg's extensive contributions to the physiological literature:

The injection of a large dose of tubocurarine (a paralysing agent used by South American Indians in their blowpipes—tube curare—and later used by anaesthetists to induce muscular relaxation during anaesthesia) caused the cat to jump 'from the table to the floor and then straight into its cage, where it started calling more and more noisily whilst moving about jerkily... During the next few minutes, the movements became wilder... Finally the cat fell with legs and neck flexed, jerking in rapid clonic movements, the condition being that of a major (epileptic) convulsion... Within a few seconds the cat got up, ran for a few yards at high speed and fell in another fit. The whole process was repeated several times within the next 10 minutes, during which the cat lost faeces and foamed at the mouth.' The animal died of respiratory failure 35 minutes after the brain injection.[5]

In another series of conscious cat experiments, propyl-benzilylcholine mustard was injected into the ventricles of the brain with the following effects:

> Shivering began within a minute or two and quickly became vigorous and widespread. The next effect was vocalisation. It began with periods of miaowing which became more frequent and of longer duration. Gradually the miaowing changed to growling and yelping. Later, tachypnoea [rapid breathing], panting, salivation, pilo-erection and ear twitching were observed... During the periods of excitation, the cats would suddenly charge blindly ahead, or jump up and cling to the side or roof of the cage, the pupils being maximally dilated. The cats showed compulsive biting ... bouts of scratching became very intense, often wounding the skin at the side and front of the ears.[6]

For at least forty years Feldberg and his various co-workers had been performing similar brain experiments. In 1965 he published an article naming 33 substances which he and others had injected into conscious cats' brains and listed the subsequent effects on the cats.[7]

In 1983 the RSPCA had included the propylbenzilylcholine mustard experiment (see above) in a report to the Home Secretary in which medical, veterinary and other experts agreed that the degree of pain, suffering or distress was substantial and that:

the only stated aim of Feldberg's experiment was to see whether the substance produced effects in cats like those already observed in rats... However, no therapeutic use was attributed to propylbenzilylcholine mustard in the published paper...*such distress would be hard to justify, even for research into problems of life-threatening diseases.*[8]

I, my medical family and friends wrote to the Home Office and to the Home Office Inspectorate from 1985 onwards but we were informed coldly that all was well. I reported his research to various anti-vivisection societies, some of whom already knew of it; there had been many demonstrations, over the years, outside Mill Hill. Dr Vernon Coleman, a medically qualified writer, wrote about the experiments in the national press, but to no avail.

In 1986 I discovered to my horror that Feldberg, now eighty-six years old, had just been given a further three-year grant by the Medical Research Council (funded by the taxpayer) to continue his research which was to involve the use of 240 cats. His experiments had therefore been endorsed by the most prestigious medical research funding body in the country, despite the fact that it was feeling the economic pinch. An article in the British Medical Association *News Review* (September 1986, p 21) stated that 'the total number of (MRC) project grants in 1984-85 had to be pruned by 19 per cent.' What could be done in the face of such official complacency and scientific approval?

In January 1988 I received a telephone call from London which changed everything. It was from Melody MacDonald, a former fashion model. She had been given my name by an animal welfare society and she said she wanted to help animals in any way she could.

After months of telephoning each other, exchanging information on many different animal welfare issues and feeling increasingly frustrated by lack of progress in any field, she announced one day, as only Melody could, that she was going to telephone Professor Feldberg.

I wished her luck but did not really believe that she would dare to telephone him or, even if she did, despite being very well spoken, that she would get any further than the secretary who would say that he was too busy to speak to her. Life, however, is full of surprises. She telephoned me within an hour to say she had been invited to lunch at his laboratory at Mill Hill!

After Melody had visited Feldberg in his laboratory several times and had observed what appeared to be numerous breaches of laboratory protocol, plus his gruesome ritual of cutting the hearts out of still living cats and rabbits, I realised that she desperately needed video-taped evidence as proof—but who could do it? It had to be done properly by someone who not only had a video camera but also a scientific training.

Very soon—within a couple of weeks—Fate came to our aid. An envelope arrived from Melody containing assorted information and included a photocopy of a letter from Mike Huskisson in which he mentioned that he filmed for animal welfare and had recently established the Animal Cruelty Investigation Group. I telephoned him and on hearing the facts he immediately offered to go anywhere, any time.

At long last it was all coming together. The rest has made history and belongs to these two courageous people who have furthered the anti-vivisection cause immeasurably.

Meanwhile, from the Home Office Inspectorate...

'Many antivivisectionist journals and leaflets contain photographs and descriptions of research which took place outside the United Kingdom and was therefore not subject to the controls here. In other cases, readers are needlessly distressed by suggestions that work is performed without anaesthesia or analgesia; that particular procedures are painful when anyone with medical knowledge could tell them that they are not; or that particular pieces of research are useless just because their purpose may not be clear to a non-scientist. This irresponsible and sometimes malicious propaganda does nothing to contribute to the elimination of avoidable suffering by animals used in research, which is the aim of the Government and of researchers themselves.'

[Personal Communication from Tony Moore, E Division, Home Office Inspectorate, December 1987.]

However, *this* book contains photographs and descriptions of research which took place inside the United Kingdom and *was* therefore subject to the controls here. Readers will be distressed to know that the work *was* performed, on several occasions, without adequate anaesthesia; that medical doctors and veterinary surgeons have stated that some of the procedures *were* painful and that the experiments witnessed *were* unscientific, crude and useless. This responsible and honest investigation will, it is hoped, help to contribute to the elimination of the use of animals in research, which is the aim of anti-vivisectionists and of a growing number of humane researchers.

PART ONE

THE INFILTRATION

Melody MacDonald

CHAPTER ONE

Curiosity Killed the Cats

SOMEBODY ONCE SAID to me that it would be impossible for me legally to infiltrate a British vivisection laboratory and investigate—so I decided to prove them wrong. The reason it is impossible is because of the high security and secrecy surrounding these establishments. They are hidden away from the public eye so that people do not hear or see the full horror and suffering behind closed doors. I am convinced that if animal research laboratories had glass, instead of walls, the public would not tolerate vivisection.

In 1988, over a period of time, I had been sent various medical research papers by a fellow animal welfarist Jill Russell—and what I read horrified me more and more.

In particular, I was horrified by the published accounts of experiments being done on live animals by a Professor Wilhelm Feldberg, at that time aged eighty-seven, at the National Institute for Medical Research (NIMR), Mill Hill, London. He was a prestigious scientist with a host of degrees. He was elected Fellow of the Royal Society in 1947 and an honorary Fellow of the Royal College of Physicians of London in 1978. He had been awarded the CBE in 1963, the honorary MD degrees of six universities mainly in Germany, the honorary DSc of Bradford and London Universities, and the LLD of Glasgow and Aberdeen Universities.

I felt that I must meet this man and see for myself what was going on. This was going to be difficult to achieve as I was a lay person, an animal welfare campaigner and an animal lover. But I had a little scientific knowledge, coming as I did from a medical background, so I took the plunge and telephoned the Professor. After a short conversation, in which I showed interest in his work

The National Institute for Medical Research at Mill Hill, London

and his years of experience, to my surprise he invited me to lunch at the NIMR. I said I would like to write his biography. But this was only the beginning...

I telephoned a fellow animal rights campaigner, Lorraine Richter, and asked her if she would accompany me. She was amazed when I told her where we were going. Her voice went faint, but she agreed to accompany me.

A week later, on 18 May 1988, at midday, I set off—or at least attempted to. To my horror my car was hemmed in, back and front, and I was unable to move it. I waited and waited for the owner to return, thinking that this stupid incident might well wreck my chances of entering a British vivisection laboratory as I would miss my appointment. However, after twenty minutes a very apologetic man arrived saying he had been at a funeral so I could hardly justifiably show my annoyance! I drove off, picked up Lorraine, and away we sped.

I cannot fully describe our feelings of dread as we neared the Institute. It was situated on top of the hill, resembling a German *schloss*. Towering on the horizon, the building filled me with foreboding. This place was the flagship of medical research in Britain. My mind raced, my hands tensed on the steering wheel— soon we would be inside this dreaded place. As we drove up the hill, I had a compulsion to turn back—but on I drove. This feeling was to haunt me on subsequent visits.

On arrival, we parked the car away from the building but suddenly realised that my car was covered in animal rights stickers such as the BUAV slogan 'Every six seconds an animal dies in a British laboratory'. This would certainly have given the game away! We removed the stickers and walked from the car up the drive of the Institute. As we approached the main door we noticed the two closed circuit cameras and bowed our heads. We climbed the steps and entered.

There was a lady seated at the reception desk so I said we were guests of Professor Feldberg. We duly signed the visitor's book with our own names. I always used my real name because I knew this would ultimately add credence and respectability to my investigation.

We were issued with security passes and after five minutes a man appeared, smiled, shook hands and introduced himself as

---

NIMR
Visitors Pass
Issued
MAY   Number **48**

'We were issued with security passes'

John Stean. He said, 'Prof is waiting for you downstairs.' Mr Stean led us through some doors and down into the bowels of the building. The Department we arrived at was marked 'Department of Pharmacology' and we were taken into the first laboratory on the right.

An old man with white hair, a white coat and gold-rimmed spectacles greeted us with outstretched hand and smiled. This was the famous Professor Wilhelm Feldberg. He was a slight man of medium height, with a stoop, a strong German accent and impeccable manners. The room was tiny, rather dark and shabby, with old equipment and a great number of books on shelves. It was hot and rather claustrophobic with little natural daylight.

The Professor beckoned us to sit down and as we did so I noticed a beautiful, large, ginger, lop-eared rabbit in a cage. He asked if we would like to watch an experiment and have lunch in the laboratory. We agreed.

Lorraine had suddenly gone decidedly pale at the prospect but I had briefed her not to show any emotion and to keep calm at all times. However she had not expected to witness an experiment and was wondering how she would cope with it. She said to me later that, being a passionate cat lover, had it been a cat in the cage instead of the poor rabbit, she could not have remained in the laboratory.

We had some cheese sandwiches which we politely forced down our dry, nervous throats, and then the experiment started. The conscious rabbit was taken out of its cage, a substance was injected intravenously and blood samples were taken from its ears every twenty minutes. Between these samples it was returned to its cage.

Apart from the obvious fear and discomfort the rabbit was forced to endure, it was a very mild experiment compared to ones I was to witness at later dates.

Professor Feldberg was a medical graduate. However, animal experimenters are, in 80 per cent of cases, people with neither a medical nor a veterinary degree. Many have a PhD degree (Doctor of Philosophy) and the public are frequently confused by this use of the title 'Doctor', and assume that the scientists are medically qualified when they are not.

Along with its sheer futility, one of my main criticisms of vivisection is that the perpetrators usually have no veterinary qualifications and no formal training in anaesthesia, analgesia, euthanasia, etc. If caught operating on animals outside the confines of a laboratory which is licensed by the Home Office, they would be prosecuted under the Protection of Animals Act (1911). But behind closed doors and under licence they are protected by the Animals (Scientific Procedures) Act 1986, which seems to me a curious anomaly.

As the day wore on we chatted to the Professor and John Stean, his laboratory technician, who had been brought out of retirement and reinstated to help him. It transpired that Professor Feldberg had had to leave Germany suddenly in 1933 following his dismissal when Hitler came to power.[9] He had originally gone to Cambridge to work with Sir Henry Dale, the famous pharmacologist, then after eleven years he had come to work at the NIMR and had stayed ever since.

His first published experimental work[10] was on frogs, written while he was still a medical student. Since then he had performed experiments on all sorts of animals over the years, including work on cobras in Australia.

Professor Feldberg was confident of his own ability, with a dry sense of humour. When I told him that I had looked him up in *Who's Who* he was flattered. I asked him why he had been awarded two LL.D degrees. He said he had no idea and sent John Stean off to the Institute library to borrow a copy of *Who's Who*. He returned with it and the Professor said he still had no idea, it must be a mistake!

He apologised for the experiment he was doing, *only* being one done on a rabbit, but his eyes lit up as he exclaimed, 'I'm getting *cats* next week—if I could breed them for research in my garden I

19

would, because they're so expensive—£130 each!' He continued, offering us a chocolate Kit-Kat, 'Some of my experiments are done on conscious animals and some on unconscious animals, but they don't suffer much.' This was to be proved to the contrary later on. 'I've used guinea pigs, monkeys, dogs and most species but cats are best because the consistency of their tissue is most like that of a human.' This however was to be contradicted by a leading vet, amongst others, at a later date.

As this particular experiment which he was conducting involved the measurement of blood sugar levels, Lorraine asked him if he had heard of Dr Max Gerson, MD, who had left Germany at about the same time, and had gone to America. He had tremendous success in curing people of tuberculosis, cancer and diabetes by strict diet. Professor Feldberg said he had never heard of him and declared that 'rabbits only eat vegetables anyway.' 'Exactly!' said Lorraine, 'and they don't get diabetes naturally,' but he did not appear to understand the significance of the remark and it fell on deaf ears.

She then asked if he had heard of Dr Vernon Coleman, another medical doctor who had written anti-vivisection newspaper articles about the Professor, but he told her that he was not shown detrimental articles about himself. In fact he said that he did not read newspapers or other people's research papers as they were boring! He then asked us point blank if we were anti-vivisectionists to which I just smiled sweetly. He showed us his many research papers and gave us some to keep, saying, 'Help yourself.'

As the day wore on and the experiment continued, the poor rabbit's ears were punctured with needles by Professor Feldberg, while his hands shook incessantly and he muttered that his eyesight and memory were failing slightly.

Neither he nor John Stean wore gloves or masks, and there was no apparent sterilisation. The laboratory door was wide open and the corridor was very noisy, with trolleys going past and people passing by, which was most disconcerting.

At one point I asked if he knew Professor Colin Blakemore,

who has a reputation for being a leading vivisector at Oxford University. He said he did, and then gave me a written introduction to him, much to our amusement. However, when I asked if we could visit the NIMR Animal House, it appeared that the security there was strict and, although the Professor was all for us seeing inside, internal telephone calls unfortunately drew a blank. So I never actually managed to see inside the NIMR Animal House, which apparently at the time held about 50,000 animals and is one of the largest in Britain dealing with animals for medical research.

We made several visits to the staff tea-room during the course of the day and saw some extraordinary people there. The room was grubby, with cracked cups, unwashed mugs and general sloppiness. On one occasion, as I walked out, I practically bumped into someone who was carrying a white rat which was bleeding from its mouth. It really gave me quite a fright.

After hours in the claustrophobic laboratory with the Professor pottering about and John Stean hovering in the background, the Professor said he was going to kill the rabbit and asked whether I wanted to watch. Lorraine asked if she could take it home instead but he said it was against the law. She left the room at this point, unable to carry on the charade.

The Professor got a syringe full of a deadly dose of Nembutal which he tried to inject into the rabbit's ear, but it was so badly damaged by the previous repetitive injections that he could not manage it. As an alternative, he plunged the syringe into the rabbit's side.

I will never forget the look in that poor creature's eyes—it was staring at me, not uttering a sound but struggling. The rabbit however did not stop breathing, so he administered more Nembutal into its ear. Eventually it died and the Professor said, 'I'm going to cut its heart out. Do you want to watch?' I tried, but after the first incision I turned away sickened, and declined his invitation to watch.

I asked him why he performed this seemingly macabre ritual

and he said it was to make sure the animal was completely dead. Subsequently when the RSPCA were asked about this they said that they thought it must be some kind of joke—but it was no joke.

The corpse and heart were put in a large yellow incinerator bag and left on the floor for collection.

I noticed that the Professor did not appear to wash his hands either during or after the experiment. He took off his white coat, put on his jacket and asked if we would like to go back to his house for tea or a drink. He said he had a book which he had written and would like to give us each a copy. We left the Institute through a side door, still wearing our security badges, and went to the car. Lorraine and I just hoped that no-one we knew had seen us. What would they have thought?

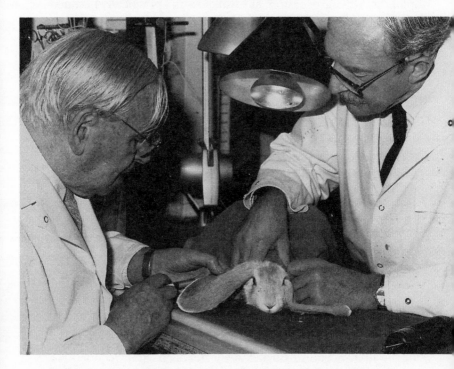

'[Feldberg's] hands shook incessantly and he muttered that his eyesight and memory were failing slightly'.

We then followed the Professor, first to the station to drop off John Stean, and then back to the Professor's home. I took a photograph of him on the doorstep and then we entered.

The Professor's house was lifeless and dark but with good antique furniture and rugs, and Toulouse-Lautrec paintings on the walls, which he told us he had bought for a song, pre-war, in Germany. As I looked round the room, a thought struck me. I wondered, 'What do the neighbours think of Professor Feldberg? I wonder if they know what he does every working day of his life?' He said he had been burgled three times and all his silver had been taken, so nowadays he left a note for the burglars which said, 'Only stainless steel left!'

He was full of jokes and a dry sense of humour which was not always easy to interpret—such as, 'Students never learn any-thing—even after eleven years—as they change every three years.' As the kitchen electricity was off, he invited us out for tea. We declined, so he gave us sherry instead. He presented us with his small black book, *Feldberg—Fifty Years On*, duly signing our copies and insisting that we sat down and read the first and last paragraphs. The last paragraph read, '*How fortunate are those who can do research their whole life. For however long they live—they die young.*'[11]

After chatting for about an hour we bade him farewell and off we went. We were both quite stunned by the experience and when asked later that evening what I thought we had gained, I replied, 'If one can continue visiting the laboratory, gain his confidence, and then *bring the truth* of what is going on to the public's attention, *that* is the point—so that the public will finally realise what goes on behind closed doors.'

Following that initial visit I certainly gained Professor Feldberg's confidence, telephoning him regularly. I paid some further visits to his laboratory, spending the whole day witnessing his experi-ments. I lunched with him there or in the NIMR canteen, and chatted to him at his home.

MY SECOND VISIT to the laboratory was just a few weeks after my initial visit with Lorraine but this time I was on my own. I was naturally rather nervous, wondering whether I would be able to continue this masquerade, and what the consequences might be.

I arrived soon after 9 am and went through the same procedure as before. However, this time a beautiful young black cat was stretched out on the operating table, its paws tied down with string. It had already been anaesthetised by the NIMR vet. The cat was kept under anaesthetic all day long during which time the Professor took me to the MRC canteen for lunch, leaving John Stean in charge of the cat.

As we walked to the canteen, along endless corridors, everyone that we passed greeted the Professor warmly and I soon realised how popular and respected he was—partly, I suspected, because he had been at the Institute for over fifty years. I managed to choose some vegetarian fare which I forced down politely, and as we ate we discussed science and medicine.

Eventually we returned to the laboratory, the Professor shuffling slowly alongside me, due to bad arthritis. The experiment on the cat resumed, taking blood samples to measure blood sugar levels, and after a couple more hours the poor creature finally died before the experiment had reached its conclusion. Professor Feldberg did not know why—it had just given up the ghost— another wasted life.

Although I found this experiment unpleasant, it was extremely mild in comparison to the experiments he had performed on conscious cats from the nineteen-fifties onwards at least until the mid-nineteen-eighties, but never during my visits to his laboratory.

Professor Feldberg told me the names of many other scientists in Britain who were or are doing similar animal brain research. I was interested to hear that most of them had worked with him at some time.

When I showed interest in his previous work he dug out an old black and white cine film[12] of some of his research on conscious cats, which he had made in the early fifties to show to fellow

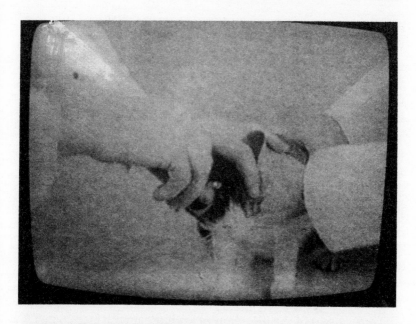

Stills from Feldberg's own film of brain experiments conducted on conscious cats in the 1950s

physiologists and students, and he gave it to me. When I watched it later, I was quite sickened by the contents.

The film showed excerpts from several experiments. The first was on a lovely tabby cat which was fully conscious, with a cannula already implanted in its skull. It had been given an injection of d-tubocurarine and was terribly distressed. It was incontinent, howling, salivating profusely and going round and round in demented circles with its fur standing on end (pilo-erection) until it dropped to the floor of the cage in a frenzied epileptic fit. This happened twice. The injections were apparently given once or twice weekly.

In a scientific paper[5] which described similar experiments using this drug, Professor Feldberg poses the question, 'Is the cat in a state of awareness during the d-tubocurarine convulsions?' He then states, 'It is not possible to define the state of consciousness in a cat...'

Another part of the film showed a white cat with black patches and a black tail. Following an intraventricular injection of DFP (diisopropylfluorophosphonate) it was in a state of catatonia. It had been placed upright on the cross-bars of an inverted stool and it stayed in any position in which it was placed for about 10 minutes or until it was eventually pushed off.

The intraventricular cannula was subsequently illustrated in detail and the operation for its insertion into the brain was demonstrated. A black cat (it looked dead—it is certainly to be hoped that it was at least anaesthetised) had a large triangular piece of fur and skin from its skull peeled back over its neck. A crude hand drill was then used to bore the hole through the bone.

Yet a further section of the film showed the researchers with another cat lying on its back on a table. The cat's front legs were contorted until they were behind its neck. It was then pulled up from a lying position by one front leg and was generally prodded and poked out of apparent curiosity and fascination as it lay in a state of helplessness after an intraventricular injection of adrenaline.

What a pity that this film could not have been shown to the public at that time.

EARLY ON IN my investigation I realised that I needed witnesses to Feldberg's experiments. I contacted some leading animal welfarists but no-one seemed to be in a position to help me. Certainly my situation was so unique and incredible that I wondered if they really believed me or whether they thought I was not *bona fide*. However I did learn that quite a few people in authority were concerned about Professor Feldberg's experiments. In desperation I then contacted the prominent Central Television investigative programme, *The Cook Report*, and visited them in Birmingham. By now Professor Feldberg had invited me to dinner. I asked if I could bring a girlfriend. He agreed. She was in fact a researcher for *The Cook Report*.

We met the Professor at the Swiss Centre in Leicester Square, and had an excellent dinner with him. Throughout the meal he discussed his work, not interested in our lives at all, fortunately, but totally obsessed with his research. I was surprised and disappointed afterwards to discover that the conversation had not been recorded.

The producer was eager to do an exposé, but the apparently insuperable problem was—how could we film? After all, British animal laboratories are notoriously secretive, and how could we possibly smuggle in a camera crew…?

As the months ticked by I managed to make a few further visits to the Professor's laboratory. I always telephoned him beforehand to make an appointment. On one visit I apparently just missed an animal rights demonstration outside Mill Hill. If anyone had recognised me, it could have blown my cover!

Over the months I was horrified to witness experiments on anaesthetised cats, mutilated beyond recognition by the end of the experimental session which usually lasted at least until mid-afternoon, depending on how soon the poor animal died. One in particular I remember, a pathetic little two-year-old black cat which just stuck in my mind's eye for days afterwards. I said a prayer for it that night.

What a waste, I thought, to breed these beautiful animals for experimentation and then to mutilate and kill them. All done in the name of 'science' or 'medical research' in the faint hope that there might be some great medical break-through. In reality this is not the case, despite over two hundred years of animal experimentation. Many great men including Albert Schweitzer and Lord Dowding have denounced vivisection as an evil practice.

At last, on 8 November 1989, I had a stroke of luck. My friend and confidant Dr Michael W. Fox, a fully qualified British veterinary surgeon now working in America where he is Vice-President of the Humane Society of the United States, was in London. He agreed to visit Professor Feldberg with me. Armed with his camera we set off on our mission.

When we arrived, a tabby cat was already anaesthetised and stretched out on its back on the operating table, with its legs tied down with string. It was on a ventilator (an artificial respirator) and its shaved abdomen was being heated by an Anglepoise lamp. Laboratory thermometers were on both the outside and inside of the cat's abdomen to record temperatures (which no-one appeared to write down all afternoon). The heat was excessive and it was appalling to watch as the abdomen was burned.

Michael questioned the Professor as to why this seemingly bizarre experiment was being performed. He was told that some weeks previously the same hot lamp had fallen accidentally on to an unattended (which was against the regulations) anaesthetised cat and had burned its abdomen. As a consequence the Professor had found that its blood sugar levels were raised. This fascinated him—although the fact that stress of all types, including all kinds

Right: 'Laboratory thermometers were on both the outside and inside of the cat's abdomen to record temperatures (which no-one appeared to write down all afternoon)'.

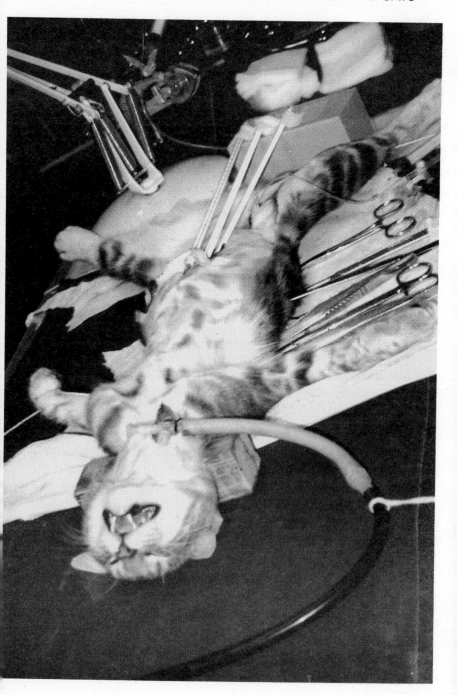

of injury and burns, could raise the blood sugar had been discovered decades previously. Subsequently we found out that his project licence did not cover this procedure.

During the afternoon Michael, horrified by the conditions, took several colour photographs of the cat and Professor Feldberg—one of which has been extensively used as a backdrop on television and in newspaper articles.

Michael then noticed that when the Professor cut open the cat's abdomen, the abdominal splanchnic nerves had not been severed as they were supposed to have been at the beginning of the experiment, with the consequence that the whole point of the experiment had been lost anyway.

Towards the end, after the cat had been cut to ribbons by incisions all over its body, John Stean put a syringe of Nembutal on the table for Professor Feldberg to euthanase the cat, but the Professor had already begun cutting out its heart. The cat gasped terribly. John Stean remarked, 'Oh, you're doing a *live* dissection today, Prof!' Unperturbed he continued, much to our horror, and then finally, mercifully, the life went out of the poor animal... But what a waste. Life is never sacred in the hands of the vivisector.

Over the months of being the guest of Professor Feldberg, I had realised that he was a law unto himself. He had been at the Institute for so long that no-one dared challenge him, which was lucky for us. He came and went as he pleased and entertained whomsoever he wished.

However, I had noticed a gradual deterioration in his health. Old age, not surprisingly, was catching up on him. Afterwards I discovered that it was by no means the exception to be elderly and still undertaking research. In June 1990 there were, in Britain alone, one hundred and twelve researchers over the age of sixty-five including four between eighty and eighty-five years old. Fortunately, as you will see in Chapter 7, the Home Office has since brought in an upper age limit of seventy years for researchers holding project licences, although they may still hold personal licences.

As autumn turned to winter I became despondent. I knew things were not right in Professor Feldberg's laboratory, but how to prove it was not easy. At this time we possessed only a few photographs, and no-one seemed able to help. Then a friend, a stalwart animal rights campaigner, gave me a newsletter from someone called Mike Huskisson, an experienced undercover investigator, which I included in an envelope of information to Jill. She immediately telephoned him and he contacted me.

I was delighted when he agreed to help, so I arranged another meeting with the Professor. I explained that my friend Dr Michael Fox, by now back in America, had asked us to film British animal research to show to students in the USA. The Professor thought it over and agreed for us to go ahead.

CHAPTER TWO

Getting it Taped

THE FIRST VISIT to the laboratory with Mike Huskisson, on 7 December 1989, was a gruelling experience. We were both very nervous in case someone walking along the corridor were to look into the laboratory and be alerted to the filming. However, we were soon comforted by the total lack of suspicion, and Mike just let the video camera roll all day long. He also took many still photographs including one of the Professor and John Stean posing together.

There was, once again, a tabby cat already anaesthetised by the NIMR vet, lying on its back on the table. Its paws were tied down and thermometers had been inserted into its shaved abdomen. It was similar to the procedure which I had witnessed with Michael Fox. The cat was on a ventilator and had had some abdominal nerves cut; its abdomen was heated and blood sugar measurements were taken.

Professor Feldberg kept referring to the cat as 'Her Majesty'. When asked why, he said it was 'as thanks to the cat' (for letting him experiment on her).

By mid-afternoon the Professor said he did not want the cat to die just then as 'the dinner is not ready yet'—referring to the heated cat—but it died unexpectedly despite his wishes. Once more they did not know the actual cause of death.

The Professor cut the cat's chest open with scissors and cut the heart out. I could not watch but asked if he had done so. He said, 'Yes, do you want it?.' I replied with sickly sarcasm that I wasn't very hungry. The dead cat and its severed heart were then dumped into a yellow plastic incinerator bag to await collection.

Afterwards, the Professor, John Stean, Mike and I went to a

café in Mill Hill for tea and cream cakes. I could hardly eat or drink after watching that experiment, but had to make the effort in order to appear at ease. We exchanged small talk and eventually dropped John Stean off at the station at the end of the road, then drove the Professor home.

Later, while discussing what we had seen that day, Mike Huskisson wondered if Feldberg cut out the animals' hearts because he was afraid that they would come back to haunt him if he didn't!

Once we got home, the video-tape was quickly copied and hidden safely by various people. We certainly dared not risk losing the film or having it stolen.

WE VISITED THE laboratory again on 15 December 1989. A rabbit was being used in this heating experiment. The Professor couldn't remember what he had done or was going to do that day. He made numerous attempts to inject anaesthetic into the rabbit's ear vein—'Can't see, that's the trouble.' The rabbit moved and screamed when John Stean attempted to 'string it out'. Eventually it had so much anaesthetic that it required to be attached to a ventilator. Thermometers and cannulae were inserted.

The Professor then fell asleep at his desk.

At one point during the heating, the skin thermometer registered 131.5°C (the boiling point of water is 100°C), and John Stean remarked that there was a faint smell of cooking. The burned and anaesthetised (?) rabbit was later left unattended for 28 minutes while we went for lunch. We knew that this was against the regulations, so Mike slipped back to pan the camera round the empty laboratory as proof.

On our return from lunch John Stean noted that the blood vessels in the rabbit's ear had changed colour. The Professor had a look and stated that they were alright. Twenty minutes later the poor animal was dead. It all seemed to be more and more like a nightmare.

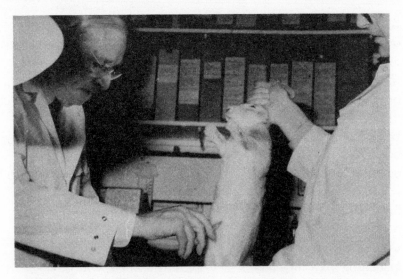

'The rabbit was held upright and stretched so that it could be anaesthetised... It cringed...'

Inserting an endotracheal cannula into the rabbit. 'It squealed piercingly while this was being done'.

AFTER EACH VISIT to the laboratory I telephoned Jill to tell her what had happened. Every time she said that she couldn't understand why on earth the Professor and John Stean thought that anyone would want to film—especially for teaching purposes—experiments which kept going wrong!

But the Professor never seemed to have any doubt that his work would be of widespread interest, and this was to be his downfall. The fact that the experiments did go wrong was, of course, the reason that Mike was able to return again and again, supposedly to obtain film of a 'successful' experiment which, in fact, never happened.

On our third visit together, on 21 December 1989, we decided to go to the laboratory early to film the entire procedure from the beginning. In a cage beside the window there was a large ginger lop-eared rabbit, just like the one that was there on my first visit with Lorraine.

The Professor was late. He had given up driving by this time 'after a few bumps', although according to the Home Office he was still considered competent to operate on live animals.

When he arrived, the rabbit was taken out of the cage, held upright and stretched by John Stean so that it could be anaesthetised by an injection into its abdomen. It cringed and John Stean stroked it.

A few minutes later, the abdomen was shaved and vacuumed, a very noisy procedure. John Stean then attempted to 'string out' the rabbit but it would not let him. It required more anaesthetic.

As the Professor cut into the rabbit's leg with a scalpel to try to insert a venous cannula, the rabbit moved again and again, struggling then screaming. This procedure which should have taken only a few minutes to complete took a horrifying twenty-four minutes.

The rabbit had a hole cut in its throat for an endotracheal tube to be inserted into its windpipe, so that it could be artificially ventilated. It squealed piercingly while this was being done.

The Anglepoise lamp was then placed over the rabbit and it

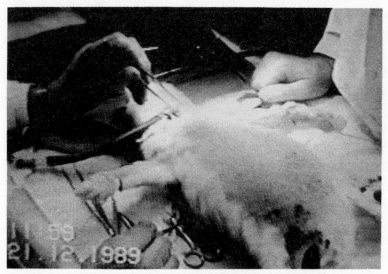

'The heated abdomen began to inflate like a balloon'.

started to heat up the abdomen. The rabbit kept lifting its head. John Stean said, 'It's a bit light,' referring to the anaesthetic, and, 'I don't think you'll get away with it, Prof.' The creature struggled violently and squeaked pathetically.

Each time the rabbit appeared to regain consciousness John Stean would keep saying, 'It's a bit light, Prof,' and eventually after an awful time lag the Professor would agree that more anaesthetic should be administered and shakily injected some into a vein in its ear.

In all the experiments we witnessed there appeared to be few if any attempts to monitor the level of consciousness by any of the many well established techniques which are used in veterinary anaesthetic practice. It was hard to believe that this was the twentieth century.

The heated abdomen began to inflate like a balloon. I could hardly contain my gasps of horror but I knew I must keep calm at all costs.

John Stean eventually noticed what was happening. The two

of them were fascinated by their experiment, postulating as to what might be the cause of the distension. They said they had no idea why this had happened.

'Something must be leaking,' said John Stean.

The scene appalled us and one felt the decent thing to do would be to save the poor creature from any further experimentation and blow our cover. However, there was too much at stake to do this so we continued the charade, giving each other sideways glances while Mike continued to film the desperate scene.

Quite soon the rabbit died. Apparently the extreme heat of the lamp had literally cooked it.

At this point Feldberg said, 'It's a dead cat.' Mike corrected him, 'It's a rabbit.'

The Professor cut it open to deflate it and to seek and cut out the heart. He did not perform a post mortem examination to find out what had gone wrong. He then seemed to become bored and asked when the next experiment was.

During the conversation afterwards in the laboratory, the Professor said that he had made a plea to the Almighty that if he had to come back as an animal, it would not be as a rabbit. John Stean said, 'I thought you were going to say, not as a cat.' The Professor and Stean laughed when I commented, 'Maybe you will come back as a cat and end up in your own laboratory.'

CHAPTER THREE

The Home Interview

IN EARLY JANUARY 1990 Mike Huskisson and I filmed an interview with the Professor at his home, on the day after he had received the Wellcome Gold Medal from the British Pharmacological Society, at the age of eighty-nine.

We had decided to go to his home because the laboratory was extremely noisy, with all its equipment, and the rattling of passing trolleys in the corridor.

Professor Feldberg had previously mentioned that a former colleague would be arriving to stay with him over New Year. We pondered over the idea of interviewing her as well, but decided against it, in case she became suspicious.

So, after lunch on 5 January 1990, we drove to Professor Feldberg's house. Mike set up the camera and the Professor settled himself in an armchair with a rug over his knees. Anyone witnessing this scene would have labelled him as a gentle old grandfatherly figure who would not harm a fly, but we knew better—he had a licence to kill.

The interview took over an hour and it was certainly interesting. He was quick-witted and jocular, and obviously flattered by all the attention. He seemed to enjoy being interviewed by me and he rose to the occasion, reminiscing about his long career and life. He still had a very strong German accent and spoke in rather broken English.

Early on, I questioned him about his cat experiments. He replied, 'I would be careful—antivivisectionists—I mean seriously—a picture—they would use that in their pamphlets; I mean I wouldn't mind but it wouldn't be very politically wise for me.' I asked if he still did conscious cat experiments. 'Yes', was the reply, although Mike and I never saw one performed. When asked later about the purpose of this work, he replied, 'There is no ultimate goal.'

I asked if he had ever had pets. 'Yes, dogs.'

We asked why he had received the Wellcome Gold Medal. He joked that he didn't know. Maybe they had made a mistake, or had no-one better or that, 'if you live long enough, these things happen.' We admired the medal which was in an acrylic block. Humorously, he wondered if it was real gold and if he could melt it down. Mike said it might just be chocolate inside!

The Professor said that he did not know if his new project licence had come through—'I can't be bothered about these things.' He said, revealingly, that he didn't know what changes the 1986 Animals (Scientific Procedures) Act contained and that if his licence were not renewed he would cheat by backdating the experiments. On further questioning about the 1986 Act he said, 'I don't know which one it is. I can't tell you. I only know I haven't read a book of rules.' He thought that his technician would draw his attention to any changes.

Regarding Home Office Inspectors—'They come from time to time. We try to stay within the law. I have never had any difficulties. I don't take the problem seriously… They ask what you are doing, ask to see your licence and discuss whether what you are doing on cats couldn't be done on rats.' He told us he never used mice or rats because he preferred cats.

'The Inspectors don't come to watch an experiment and I don't avoid them because if a cat or rabbit is anaesthetised, it is anaesthetised…and if I expect an Inspector coming and do an experiment I would naturally give a full anaesthetic dose so they cannot say it is not anaesthetised—but normally I would do that—but when they are there I am more careful.' He thought it was years since he had seen an Inspector. 'I don't take them so seriously.'

He said he had had a good result in September with a rabbit—'more to my surprise.' Certainly *we* were more than surprised when he said that he considered the present experiments to be successful! He continued, 'I haven't got the right anaesthetic for rabbits. I am not (as) happy with my anaesthetic for rabbits as I am for cats. I have more accidents with rabbits than with cats. I don't know what it is. When a rabbit died early, I took Stean out for lunch. I can't take it seriously.'

Experts had told me that Sagatal was not the anaesthetic of choice for rabbits. I therefore asked him if there was a more modern anaesthetic than Sagatal. He said he didn't know.

Regarding the length of time taken for rabbit vein injections nowadays, he replied, 'I don't take the problem seriously.' He gave the same reply when questioned about the price of animals.

I asked if a television monitor in the laboratory would help when they left the animal alone for a coffee break. He said, 'No, once they are under, they're under—there is no need to monitor when we are out of the room.'

Regarding his book, *Fifty Years On*, I asked him what he had discovered in the last fifty years. He opened a copy of the book which was lying on a table beside him and said, 'Work on nettles at Cambridge.' (He had worked on histamine from nettle stings).

After about half an hour he offered us some delicious German biscuits and I made tea for the three of us. The Professor said, 'I visit Germany twice a year—my family has property there. I come back with money, you see, because I'm an idealist who likes money.'

He said his grants were mainly from the MRC. 'I write a report every year for the MRC. Everyone has to... whether they [the MRC] have to read it is one question, whether they do is another. The taxpayer's money is well used.'

I asked what was the purpose of his work regarding the heating of the animal's abdomen. His answer—'To get more information on the effect of heat on human bodies.'

I asked if we can extrapolate the results to humans. He replied, '*I don't like to answer that because I don't know.*' He said he didn't expect anyone to carry on his work once he finished. He also said he should read more of other people's papers, but he found it so boring.

To my mind the interview was rather amateurish as I was inexperienced. It was not helped by the housekeeper, in another room, cheerfully shouting to remind him that 'Pyke is coming to tea.' Dr David Pyke was a co-author of several of Feldberg's more recent research papers, and according to the Professor they were still doing an experiment together once a week at the MRC.

The housekeeper continued, in her strong Cockney accent, 'I've laid the table for Pyke, he's coming for tea later on'—she laughed—'such a busy life! Bye bye, Prof, bye bye.' The interview was interrupted a few minutes later, at another crucial point, when she returned announcing that she had forgotten her handbag.

I asked if he had ever met any anti-vivisectionists. He said, 'Not many.' He said he was not frightened of them—'I just ask if they are vegetarians. If they are, at least they are consistent. If you eat animals, why not experiment on them? Man was created in the image of God and *not mere little-tittle pussy cats.*'

I enquired if there were any new medical implications from his work for people suffering from diabetes. 'I can't answer that.'

I asked if his colleagues read his papers. 'I don't mind, so long as they are quoted—I really can't tell you. Once a paper is written, it doesn't interest me any more...by nature I like to show off.'

When we had finished, we asked him to sign a short copyright document which we had been advised to do by one of the television producers from the television documentary programme, *World in Action*. The Professor read it out loud and as he signed it he added, presumably as a joke, '...and allow them to publish anything in the *anti*-vivisection papers they want.' We nearly froze when he said this! But little did he know...

MIKE, ALTHOUGH BUSY with other projects, made four more visits to the laboratory to continue with the collection of documentary evidence to prove breaches of the 1986 Act (see Part Two).

On every visit it was obvious that things were really seriously amiss and that what was happening must at all costs be publicised.

World in Action had already been contacted. They were very interested in doing a programme but finally after prolonged deliberation they decided against it, as their policy is to do their own filming. This was disappointing, as Mike eventually managed to shoot well over 30 hours of video-tape, containing damning evidence, which we knew the public must see.

The Animals (Scientific Procedures) Act 1986 was by now coming into force. Although he said that he was still licensed for the conscious brain research on cats which he had been doing for decades, Feldberg was observed using only anaesthetised cats and inadequately anaesthetised rabbits.

Mike therefore did not have the opportunity to film the conscious cat brain research although, as has already been said, film does exist of some of this, taken by Feldberg himself.[13] If the general public could have seen that research at the time, public pressure would almost certainly have forced such animal experimentation to stop immediately.

Later, in the Report[14] of the MRC Inquiry, it was stated that *'there were frequent concerns when cats were being used by Professor Feldberg. There was markedly less interest when he switched to rabbits.'* The real reason, of course, was that a few concerned people knew of my infiltration of the laboratory and refrained from writing to the Home Office.

With the scientific establishment and vested interests solidly ranged against us, we realised that we needed the umbrella of an anti-vivisection society to co-ordinate a public exposé. In April 1990, Mike Huskisson and I went to Edinburgh to see Les Ward at the Scottish Society for the Prevention of Vivisection (now renamed Advocates for Animals). They agreed to help to refund our expenses and organise media coverage.

Advocates for Animals submitted the video-tapes and a forty-seven page detailed report, recommending prosecutions and reprimands, to the Home Office on Thursday 3 May, 1990.

The Home Office[15] announced the following day that Professor Feldberg and John Stean had voluntarily renounced their licences to experiment on animals that very day, but that *their actions were not related to the Society's evidence*! It was, a spokesman insisted, *a mere coincidence that a career stretching back to the nineteen-thirties had ended the very day after the arrival of the critics' dossier.*[16] It was subsequently revealed that, in fact, their personal licences had been revoked immediately.[14]

Exclusive articles appeared in *The Independent* and *Glasgow Herald*. I attended a press conference at the House of Commons, and extensive newspaper reports were followed by sympathetic documentaries on the prestigious television programmes *Nature* and *Newsnight*, both of which showed parts of the video-taped evidence.

Professor Feldberg stated in the local press[17] that he had retired because of his age and that he knew nothing of the report by Advocates for Animals. He said: 'The group do not want the truth. They have a different attitude, they are fanatics. I dismiss the report 100 per cent. I do not look at animals in the same way as humans—that's the difference between them and me.' He added that he could not experiment properly unless animals were anaesthetised properly.

Predictably, the scientific establishment, rocked to the core by the exposé, reacted angrily. Amongst several irate and hostile letters published was one from some of Professor Feldberg's former colleagues[18] who wrote, having admitted that they had not even seen the video-taped evidence:

It is difficult to imagine a sorrier tale of lies, fraud and deceit... It is perhaps worthy of note that it took them a remarkably long time to obtain, or to report, any 'evidence'... We would have expected *Nature*...to have condemned out of hand the disgusting methods used to collect the 'evidence' against him, which disfigure the animal welfare movement.

They all missed the point completely.

Would I really have been invited into the laboratory if I had told the Professor the real reason? And would Mike have been allowed to film the experiments?

In fact, Mike and I had been invited to the laboratory. Visits with Mike Huskisson revealed breaches of the 1986 Act, laboratory protocol and Professor Feldberg's personal and project licences. One factor affecting the length of the investigation was that Professor Feldberg was working only part-time. However, the main reason was the absence of video-taped evidence until Mike offered to help.

Many people had complained on *numerous* occasions over *many* years about Professor Feldberg's research and were assured that all was well. Mike filmed *with permission* and the film *has* been shown to students. *No* experiment we attended ever reached Feldberg's desired conclusion. Most importantly of all, *if nothing had been amiss there would have been nothing to expose.* Certainly the animal welfare movement has not been disfigured—quite the contrary.

When I first visited the laboratory on 18 May 1988, little did I know what was to be the outcome. Almost two years later, on 6 May 1990, the long and harrowing investigation into Professor Feldberg's research would finally end. The result would be that his licence to experiment on animals was revoked by the Home Office after seventy years of animal research.

Despite initial official challenges, denials and attempted cover-ups, the exposé was acknowledged by the establishment, by parliament and by the scientific and medical community. Letters and phone calls of congratulations would ensue from numerous people, including peers of the realm, doctors and prominent MPs.

Sir Brian Bailey, chairman of the MRC Inquiry into this investigation, is quoted[19] as saying that 'this case has reverberated throughout all the animal research establishments' of the UK and that 'if there were one or two scientists who were thinking of cutting a corner, I am sure they will think differently now.' Yes. They never know when they may be 'caught in the Act'—or by whom.

PART TWO

THE CULMINATION

Animal Cruelty Investigation Group

CHAPTER FOUR

Some Rabbits do Cry

This chapter is based on the video-taped evidence collected by ACIG and transcripts prepared by Advocates for Animals

MEANWHILE, BACK IN the laboratory, even worse was to come. After the home interview, in order to complete the collection of documentary evidence, Mike Huskisson returned to the laboratory on 10 January, 1990, but this time on his own. The technician, Mr Stean, was late because he could not find anywhere to park his car. Feldberg kept asking Mike which day it was.

Once again, the experiment was on a ginger lop-eared rabbit. There was a large wicker hamper-type basket on the table. Mr Stean weighed the basket which contained the rabbit. He then took the heavily sedated rabbit out, put it on the table and, using a very noisy electric shaver, shaved its ear, ready for the administration of the anaesthetic.

He put the basket on the floor. The rabbit remained completely still on the table, wrapped in a green cloth with only its head and ears visible. Feldberg went over and injected the anaesthetic.

A surprising feature of the laboratory was the constant noise which was not at all what might have been expected in an experimental establishment. In the corridor outside the room, people were shouting, trolleys were clattering, and doors were slamming constantly.

The rabbit's abdomen was shaved and the noise of the vacuum cleaner used to remove the shaved fur then added to the general din.

At about 10 am, after 'stringing out' the rabbit, Mr Stean commented that the anaesthetic was very deep. Feldberg appeared unconcerned and replied, 'It's deep, good.' Mr Stean then had to suggest that because the anaesthetic was so deep, an endotracheal tube should be inserted immediately to assist the rabbit's breathing and 'to be on the safe side.'

Later, Feldberg used a scalpel to try to insert a cannula into a vein in the rabbit's right leg. The vein collapsed so Feldberg decided to use the vein in the left leg. He commented, 'My eyes don't see any more, that's the trouble—I can't change that.' The vein in the left leg then collapsed and Feldberg again commented on the state of his eyes. After failing to find veins in both back legs he attempted to inject into one of the jugular veins in the rabbit's neck. He failed again and commented, 'Too small for my eyes.' He then decided to try the other jugular vein.

After spending half an hour attempting to insert a venous cannula to take blood, Feldberg suddenly said, 'Wait a moment, what do we want to inject?' Mr Stean seemed surprised by this question and, after a pause, he replied, 'No, we want to *take* blood. We won't be injecting into the vein. Except the anaesthetic, that's the only thing of course. You'll need to keep one of the ears, won't you, in case we need to give more anaesthetic?'

Having failed to cannulate the other jugular vein, he decided to try the vein in the ear. He missed the vein and just punctured the skin. Mr Stean thought Feldberg should use a scalpel blade so that he could use the same puncture area each time, but he insisted on continuing to use the needle.

At about 11.30 am the anaesthetised rabbit was left completely unattended in the laboratory for nineteen minutes while Feldberg, Stean and Mike went for a coffee break. After they returned, Feldberg commented on the anaesthetised rabbit, 'It hasn't run away.' Even although the animal was completely still, Feldberg had trouble inserting thermometers into the rabbit.

The noise from the laboratory equipment was dreadful and then someone began hammering nearby. Fortunately, this rabbit was so 'deep' that it remained oblivious to the general cacophony.

Mike then questioned Mr Stean about the levels of anaesthetic.

MR STEAN: 'It's a bit of a battle with the rabbits because most of them do seem to die sometime in the afternoon. We haven't really got a satisfactory anaesthetic, that's the truth of the matter. Even the vet had difficulty with anaesthetising rabbits and someone else had started using inhalation anaesthesia, and it was more successful.'

The discussion then turned to the use of *decerebration* (destruction of part of the brain, following which the animal is supposed to live without consciousness), still widely used by vivisectors as an alternative to anaesthesia.

MR STEAN: 'Someone here worked out that the animal would still feel pain in the facial nerve and the Home Office had allowed this, but the scientist wouldn't do the work for moral reasons.'

Eventually, after having trouble taking blood by needle, Feldberg had to lance the vein. Just an hour after the coffee break, the rabbit was again left unattended while Feldberg, Stean and Mike went for lunch. Half an hour after their return, Feldberg approached the rabbit to take a further blood sample. It moved its legs and lifted its head pathetically.

MR STEAN: 'Getting a bit light now.'

But still Feldberg continued to take blood. No more anaesthetic was given. After another half hour, a further blood sample was taken and again the rabbit moved and lifted its head.

MR STEAN: 'It's light, Prof.'

The rabbit attempted to get up on several occasions but each time its head was held down by Mr Stean. Still no extra anaesthetic was given. The rabbit's head moved again but Feldberg and Mr Stean continued to try to get a blood sample.

Ten minutes afterwards, the lamp was put on the rabbit which was visibly moving its leg.

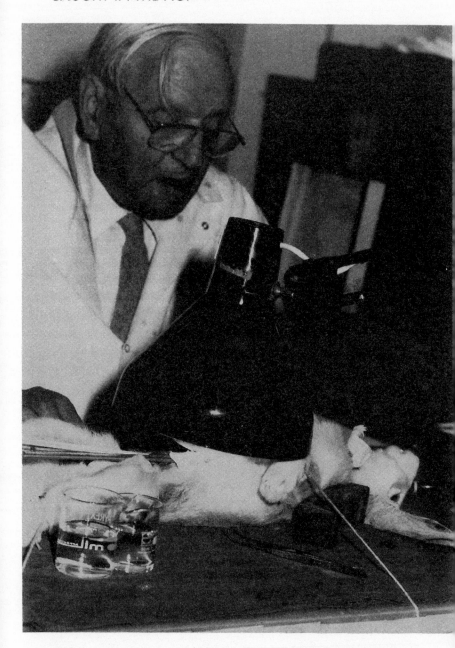

'The lamp was put on the rabbit, which was visibly moving its leg'.

MR STEAN: 'Of course it might react, Prof, because it's fairly light I think.'

The rabbit attempted to get up and the lamp was taken off. Some Sagatal was at last injected into a vein in the ear which was already damaged through previous blood sampling. Only 23 seconds after giving the anaesthetic they decided again to heat the rabbit.

Before they could get the lamp onto the rabbit it struggled so violently that it ejected the four thermometers which had been taped to its body. They scattered noisily all over the table. The thermometers were replaced and more Sagatal was injected with difficulty.

Feldberg went back to his desk to write up his book. He asked what time the lamp had been put on.

MR STEAN: 'We stopped that, Prof.'
PROFESSOR: 'We didn't do that?'
MR STEAN: 'Well, no, because you had to give more anaesthetic.'
PROFESSOR: 'What anaesthetic was that...?'

Feldberg had forgotten what had just happened. Seven minutes after this further anaesthetic had been given, the lamp was replaced over the rabbit. Yet again the creature moved.

MR STEAN: 'It's moving its head a little. It's just a question as to whether it will stand twenty minutes of this.'
PROFESSOR: 'Maybe we are going to become anatomists.'

More Sagatal was then administered and the lamp was placed directly above the rabbit's abdomen.

MR STEAN: 'I'm just wondering if we ought to raise the lamp a bit Prof... Can I just tell you that the visceral [internal organs] temperature is up to 60°C. Might kill it Prof.'

Feldberg raised his voice, ignoring Stean's words. 'When did we give it the Sagatal?' Mr Stean raised his arms in frustration.

Feldberg finally came over to have a look at the rabbit and lifted the lamp off.

MR STEAN: 'You're taking the lamp off?'
PROFESSOR: 'No, no.'
MR STEAN: 'Well, you've lifted it, Prof.'
PROFESSOR: 'Yes, just for a minute.'

The lamp was replaced after two minutes. Mr Stean again said that the visceral temperature was very high. Feldberg said, 'It is good,' and walked back to his desk.

No more anaesthetic had been given and nothing had been done in relation to the visceral temperature. The skin temperature at this time was 100°C—the boiling point of water. Mr Stean pointed out that the visceral temperature had gone off the scale. Feldberg said, 'That's all right.'

After checking that Feldberg still wanted the lamp on for twenty minutes, Stean turned to Mike, laughing, and said, 'Well, if that doesn't kill it!'

Shortly afterwards, Mike pointed out that part of the rabbit's intestines were hanging out and were directly under the heat of the lamp. After having this drawn to his attention, Stean said, 'That's a point Prof—there's a loop of intestine coming out and of course that's going to get locally very hot, isn't it?' Feldberg came over slowly and raised the lamp again.

MR STEAN: 'Oh, you're going to shift the lamp again?'
PROFESSOR: 'Only for a moment.'

It was off for three minutes and the intestine was pushed back inside. Because the lamp had been taken off and put back on again, Stean remarked that he didn't know what relevance the thermometer readings would have.

Less than ten minutes later, Mr Stean commented that 'the visceral [temperature] is so high I can't read it now Prof... No you can't estimate it because the mercury is in the little bulb at the [top] end so it must be very hot...in excess of 67°C plus, something like that.'

Seven minutes later the lamp was taken off. Burn marks were clearly visible on the rabbit's abdomen. A blood sample was again taken with difficulty. Because of the condition of the ears it took them nineteen minutes to get a 'little' blood.

Despite being aware of the Health and Safety Regulations, they decided to bring cups of tea into the laboratory. They drank them beside the rabbit.

WHAT WITH MR STEAN having flu and Feldberg visiting Germany, there was a gap of several weeks before the next visit on 30 March 1990 when Mike returned to the laboratory, to witness and film another rabbit experiment.

At about 10 am Feldberg still had not arrived in the laboratory so Mike chatted to Mr Stean. Mike asked about the hyperglycaemia which they were investigating.

MR STEAN: 'It was quite obvious from the papers I managed to dig out that they have known about this sort of thing for quite a long time, really—back in the seventies—but he wouldn't read them. I was determined. I sat down once and read one to him and he promptly went off to sleep!'

Mike then enquired about the problems they were having with anaesthetising the rabbits.

MR STEAN: 'He had a lot of problems at the beginning, yes...they were very difficult...it was very difficult to keep them under, they were either 'light' or dead. It took me ages to persuade him to use diluted anaesthetic, but he has done that and I think it has been better...the margin is so small between [the effective and] the fatal dose, and Prof is now a little impetuous when he injects things and sometimes he sort of drifts off and goes on injecting, or something happens, and he sometimes gives too much.'

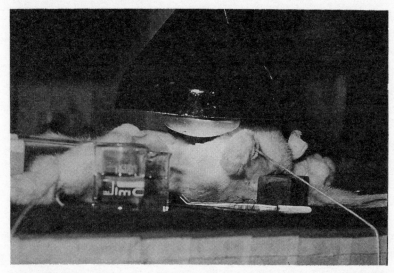

'Might kill it, Prof.'

Questions were asked about the burning aspects of the experiments.

MR STEAN: 'Yes, of course the trouble is really it's a bit beyond the Prof now, there's a limit to what he can do.'

Half an hour later Feldberg arrived and he noticed that the rabbit was panting heavily. With a surprised tone in his voice he exclaimed, 'Look at its respiration, it's over 200.' He asked the rabbit, 'Why are you so excited?' and then by way of explanation he said, 'It is frightened.'

The frightened rabbit soon attempted to escape during blood sampling. It virtually jumped straight into Mike's arms. Handing the rabbit back to the vivisectors must have been one of the hardest things that Mike has ever had to do.

Ten minutes later Feldberg injected 3 ml of phenoxybenzamine, a heart drug, and Stean informed him that it should be injected gradually over ten minutes. He then told him to slow up a bit, pointing out that, 'We should really do it for fifteen minutes.'

Feldberg, while injecting the drug, remarked that the rabbit struggled when he put in too much. He then stated, 'Five minutes instead of ten.' Stean corrected him, 'Four minutes, Prof,' and then laughed.

An hour later, just after midday, Feldberg fell asleep.

THE NEXT VISIT was on 5 April 1990. This time Mike was accompanied by Les Ward from the Scottish Society for the Prevention of Vivisection (now renamed Advocates for Animals). They were to witness and film an experiment on yet another ginger lop-eared rabbit.

When asked whether cats were a better animal for Feldberg's work and if he would get better results from them than from rabbits, Feldberg replied, 'I wouldn't say that.' Mr Stean said, 'Oh, you think it's just what we've got used to?' To which Feldberg replied, 'It is how you evaluate the results. As long as they're reliable, it's all right.'

When Stean was asked whether they had a set number of animals to use or whether they got them pretty well when they wanted them, he replied rather surprisingly that they got them 'pretty well when we want them.'

As to the possible loss of his licence to perform experiments, Feldberg responded, 'Look here, either I go on legally, if I am allowed, otherwise I go on illegally if I am not allowed, but go on I will.'

Mr Stean laughed. 'You would too, Prof.'

CHAPTER FIVE

The Last Gasp

This chapter is based on the video-taped evidence and a telephone conversation,both recorded by ACIG , and on transcripts prepared by Advocates for Animals.

MIKE'S VISIT ON 23 April 1990 was to be the last, as it produced more than enough irrefutable evidence of animal suffering to convince even the Home Office.

Mike had arrived at the laboratory just before 10 am. Whilst awaiting the arrival of Feldberg, Mike had another chat with Mr Stean. He wanted to check up on a few points.

MIKE: 'Reviewing the whole thing while we have been here, one of the things that intrigues me is how it originally started…with the lamp falling [on the cat]. Because when we said this to people, what they couldn't understand is how you got any reading. If you're working here now—boom— the light drops down and you pick it up straight away.'

MR STEAN: 'Well, it wasn't noticed. That was the thing you see—it had just fallen of its own accord.'

MIKE: 'Did this happen while you were out at lunch?'

MR STEAN: 'Well, I think we might have been behind the screen and recording the results or something…'

MIKE: 'How did it happen for long enough to get it to produce any effect?'

MR STEAN: 'Well, I can't remember how long. We wouldn't have known. One thing I noticed when he was doing the post-mortem was that the guts actually felt hot to the touch and I pointed this out to him. We measured the temperature and found it was very high. Then of course it got this

hyperglycaemia, and he sort of followed it up from there...
But the problem for Prof is that he was not prepared to read
other people's papers. Really, it wasn't a new finding at all.
It was confirmation of what people knew. In fact, I got a
text-book and read it to him.'

When discussing the use of Sagatal, Stean commented, 'We've
pretty well got it wrapped up but he did have one death the other
day. I tried to persuade him in the beginning to use diluted Sagatal
because it's much safer to do it that way, and he said, 'Oh no, I
can give it some more.' And of course he sometimes drops off to
sleep, or is half asleep while he is injecting, so he injects the
whole lot or something.'

Feldberg arrived. Another ginger lop-eared rabbit was fated to
become anti-vivisection history. It was taken out of the cage by
the scruff of its neck and wrapped in a dark green cloth to keep it
still and calm.

Once the experiment was under way, the rabbit was seen to be
moving while Feldberg was taking a blood sample from its ear.
No more anaesthetic was given.

Ten minutes later Feldberg informed Mike that he was about
to insert a tracheal cannula. Mike told him that he would have to
give more anaesthetic. 'It's a bit light.'

Feldberg replied, 'Let me have a look,' and promptly attempted
to make an incision to insert the endotracheal tube (i.e. a tube
into the windpipe) into the base of the neck.

The rabbit jumped.

Feldberg used the scalpel four other times and each time the
rabbit jumped. Feldberg then commented, 'I think we might get
it without difficulty.'

He then started using surgical scissors. As he snipped, the
rabbit moved. As he continued snipping, the rabbit was constantly
squirming and pathetically lifted its head off the table.

This continued for some time with the rabbit moving violently.

Feldberg slipped his finger into the hole he had cut in the
rabbit's neck, and he then cut out a piece of tissue. He used the

scissors again, and once more the rabbit squirmed.

More tissue was taken away. He snipped again and, not surprisingly, the rabbit attempted to get up. He snipped again and again, following which there was a frantic reaction from the rabbit.

Mr Stean, who until now had been doing a test on a blood sample taken earlier and had his back to Feldberg, at long last saw that the rabbit was moving and remarked, 'It's a bit light, Prof.'

He was ignored.

The rabbit was now struggling constantly but still Feldberg continued to cut into it with the scissors. As the endotracheal tube was tied in, the rabbit struggled violently and jumped numerous times.

Still Feldberg proceeded, with Stean watching.

As the rabbit jumped, it made strange noises. It was so conscious that it was fighting for breath against the ventilator.

During this dreadful period of six minutes no anaesthetic was given. Mr Stean pointed out that they would shortly be putting the lamp on the rabbit and suggested giving Sagatal, to which Feldberg agreed.

Half an hour later Feldberg was again having difficulty taking blood from the rabbit. Mr Stean advised him that he should make a slit and not poke the needle in the vein because that is what he believed shut it down. He then remarked, 'I think you are at the side of it Prof, I don't think you're in the vein.' The rabbit struggled. Again Feldberg was informed that he was at the side of, not in, the vein.

Mr Stean's comments were again ignored.

A few minutes later Mr Stean, dealing with a blood sample, had his back to the rabbit again. Feldberg was sitting at his desk, also with his back to the rabbit. The rabbit attempted to get up. It struggled on the table but neither researcher was aware of what was going on.

Before leaving for lunch, Mr Stean asked Feldberg if he was happy about the anaesthetic, 'before we leave.' Mike pointed out that the rabbit had moved. Mr Stean commented, 'I think it's a little on the light side possibly, Prof.'

The rabbit confirmed this by again attempting to get up. Mr Stean remarked, 'Yes, oh gosh, its getting up, Prof.' If the rabbit had not been tied down it would have been off the table. Mr Stean had to hold it down.

The poor rabbit, by now on its side despite being tied down, struggled and attempted to get up yet again as Feldberg injected more Sagatal. Mr Stean informed him that he was not in the vein. It seemed that Feldberg had injected most of the anaesthetic outside the vein. Mr Stean remarked, 'I don't think it got very much at all Prof.' A further injection of Sagatal was given.

By this time it was lunchtime and Mike asked whether the animal should be left unattended. Stean replied, 'We'll see. You've got two opposing legislations. One says you mustn't leave the animal here and the other which says you mustn't eat here... The only thing you can do is go in relays of course. Tim[?] has more or less ruled that going two doors down is not leaving the animal.'

At 1.30 pm Feldberg, Mr Stean and Mike went for lunch leaving the animal unattended. They were away for twenty-four minutes. Shortly after they returned, Feldberg fell asleep in front of the rabbit at the surgical table. Four minutes later, when he woke up, the lamp was placed above the rabbit's abdomen. Before doing this, Mr Stean remarked, 'I don't know whether it will take the heating. We'll just have to see, Prof, won't we?'

A rectal thermometer was inserted and the poor rabbit once again lifted its little head. Feldberg asked Mr Stean, regarding the lamp, 'Aren't you going to put it a little lower?' Twenty seconds later the rabbit moved and attempted to get up yet again. Mr Stean remarked, 'No, it's not going to take it, Prof.'

A few minutes later the lamp was brought down again. The rabbit moved its head slightly and when the temperature reached 80°C the lamp was raised a little. The rabbit's burned abdomen could be seen quite clearly.

The next attempt to take a blood sample took eleven minutes.

Shortly afterwards the poor rabbit died and its suffering finally came to an end.

LATER, IT WAS discovered that Feldberg and John Stean had planned to continue experimenting on rabbits, at the rate of three a week, until at least September 1990. Despite their MRC grant running out at the end of April, they had been given permission to continue making use of the NIMR laboratory and its facilities for a further five months.

Just after the last video-recorded experiment, Mike telephoned Mr Stean to clarify a few further points.

Mike asked about the extension of the use of the laboratory.

MR STEAN: 'It's a very extraordinary situation. I've never come across anything like this ever before. [He laughed.] I think it must be unique.'

Mr Stean, who had the disconcerting habit of not finishing sentences, seemed almost relieved to be able to speak frankly about the situation with Feldberg. He continued, 'It is very difficult. He is a very obstinate man. If he doesn't want to do something…it's almost impossible to move him with dynamite.'

MR STEAN: '…he was very difficult…about his grant application and, to be honest, I don't know how much liaison there is between all these different people, and committees and things, but he was really—must be honest about it—he was very naughty about his grant application… I think he had two applications sent back because they weren't really full enough. I don't think the committee considered that he had made a sufficient application…

'Between you and me, he still wouldn't do it, and in the end he agreed to my writing something which I did. He cut bits out of that because he didn't want to make a very big sort of thing about it, but in the end, he did accept a lot of the things I said, and that went forward. I think there were a few more modifications made by Tim, and that finally went up, and they wouldn't even accept that. It is difficult.

'…it might have been kinder if they'd stopped funding him, well, perhaps quite some time ago.

'He had a letter from the Home Office in March [about] which I kept on at him, but he wouldn't answer it. So he had a second one because they're not happy about some aspects of his work, and they want clarification.

'He kept putting it off but, after a lot of cajoling, I got him to write it, or he wrote a paragraph and I said to him, "Well look Prof, this isn't enough, they won't accept this, they'll only come back at you because you're not answering the questions."

'The Prof said, "I've written it in such a way that it includes all they want to know. It sort of bypasses all that." I said, "You don't understand, Prof—these are bureaucratic minds. They have a lot of power, more than they used to have you know, and goodness knows they've always been powerful. Anyway, I've got to get some sort of reply to the Home Office." '

MIKE: 'I couldn't understand why they [the Home Office] kept asking him about recovery experiments, because none of them recover...'

MR STEAN: 'I think they've got themselves a little bit muddled up.'

MIKE: 'Well it's almost as if they [the Home Office] are talking about the earlier work he did, isn't it?'

MR STEAN: 'Yes, you see they [the Home Office] said "...you've got Phentolamine on every item of your licence," and we say that the Phentolamine work has stopped, but they [the Home Office] conclude that all work on living animals has now stopped, which is...almost naive really. But then of course they're remote from it, aren't they?

'These last five years have seen a marked deterioration in him, you know, at first physically I think, and now mentally to quite a degree.

'I suppose that the truth of the matter is really...they should have stopped it, probably last autumn.'

MIKE: 'Do the Home Office Inspectors ever ask you when they come round, how things are going?'

MR STEAN: 'Well, when they come out they usually have lots of people to see. There was an inspector—it must have been at least two years ago, when we were regularly doing recovery animals. The Prof took him over to see everything—cats with the venous cannulas and everything, and the inspector commented to me afterwards, that Prof had had great difficulty in getting the needle in the cannula, you know because of his eyesight. I said well, he may appear like that but he always manages to cannulate them.

So it's a little strange, that this one, three inspectors ago, commented not on his mental ability but on his physical ability and did notice that his eyesight wasn't very good, *but neither of the later two did.*'

MIKE: 'You'd have thought as he gets into that sort of age, they'd perhaps come round more regularly—and ask you as well?'

MR STEAN: 'Yes...[but] I think he's very jealous. You know he doesn't really like people asking me questions about the work. He clearly resents it.

'I started working with him about five years ago, when he still had a good deal of his mentality left and much more of his mobility, but even then, there were little things that I met...sort of got used to them, used to steel myself to them.' (He laughed.) 'He really used to get to me.

'I used to be the Principal Technician of the Institute, which is a sort of managerial post. One minute he treats you as though you are a sort of co-author, and next minute it's just as though you were a junior technician from the fifties... From my point of view, that has been probably the most disappointing part of working with him over the last five years because so many of the sort of wrinkles and things that I've learnt, he won't accept any of them, none of them whatsoever.

'It's just that people coming in, as you have, and spending a good part of the day there, must wonder what the hell is going on...'

CHAPTER SIX

The Medical Research Council Inquiry

With comments by Advocates for Animals

AFTER THE VIDEO-tapes had been handed to the Home Office, and following the publicity, the Medical Research Council launched an official inquiry[14] into Professor Feldberg's experiments.

The summary of the inquiry findings published on 4 February 1991 included the following criticisms. Emphasis has been added.

The Animals

- Unnecessary suffering or avoidable pain was caused to four rabbits.
- 'In all cases, the situation arises from an anaesthetic being "too light." Remedial steps were taken, but not always as speedily as might be hoped for.'
- 'One, if not more, of these incidents constituted a breach of the conditions of the personal licences held by Professor Feldberg and Mr Stean for which they must be held responsible. In consequence, a breach of the conditions of the NIMR's certificate of designation occurred. The observance of those conditions is the responsibility of the certificate holder, Dr Skehel.'

Professor Feldberg

- 'When the Professor started his experiments of heating the abdomen of animals, that work was not covered by the project licence. *That was a breach of the Act.*'

63

- Professor Feldberg continued with one or two more of his heating experiments after it was drawn to his attention that the experiments were not covered by the project licence. *'That was a deliberate breach of the Act.'*

- 'On a number of occasions he failed to maintain an adequate level of anaesthetic' which 'meant that the *work was unauthorised by the project licence.'*

- 'He failed to recognise the deterioration in his own capacity to carry out intricate work of which his technician assistant was capable.'

- *'Anaesthetised animals were left unattended* during experimental procedures. There was a local dispensation permitting this, but we consider such an arrangement was wrong.'

- 'On at least one occasion he consumed refreshment in the laboratory contrary to Health and Safety rules.'

- 'The use of Sagatal was clearly indicated in the application for the project licence and was approved by the Home Office.'

Mr Stean

- 'Failed to act decisively when it was obvious to him that *adequate levels of anaesthetic were not being maintained.* Although not in a position of authority over the Professor, he is a personal licence holder and therefore has personal responsibility.'

- 'Together with the Professor, he failed to observe Health and Safety rules relating to the banning of refreshments in laboratories.'

Medical Research Council

- 'The machinery for dealing with applications for research grants did not operate satisfactorily in this case. The quality of Professor Feldberg's initial application, in sharp contrast to earlier submissions as recent as 1987, should have alerted the MRC to the current state of the Professor's faculties...'

Campaigners' video shows l...

Report tells of tortured rabbits

12 PRESS AND JOURNAL

THE body of a laboratory rabbit was shaved, then locked with a lamp about two inches from the skin, as heat was heard yesterday.

A Medical Research Council report said rabbits endured "unnecessary suffering" and died "for no discernible benefit" in experiments performed by Professor Wilhelm Feldberg (90).

It described how one animal "emits what reasonably might be described as a scream" while another appeared to be

anaesthetic were not retained, it found.

The Home Office inquiry withdrew the award of licences to carry out experiments when the Advocate Animals organisation and a video detailing the incidents.

Both men have not had have been barred from further MRC work.

Responding to the report, the Home Office Minister Angela Rumbold said think that the report

Top scientist is criticised for cruelty to animals

By THOMSON PRENTICE, MEDICAL CORRESPONDENT

A DISTINGUISHED medical scientist carried out worthless experiments on rabbits and caused them unnecessary suffering, a report published by the Medical Research Council said yesterday.

The interior controls of research involving animal experiments are to be introduced by the council after the practice of research by Feldberg, some of

company he
his operating table, remarks on
the animal's blood sugar levels. In
his weekly council should have
checked had it allowed the
a research grant to do the work
but he was allowed to

Research council failed to prevent animals' suffering

By Jack O'Sullivan

THE government-funded Medical Research Council yesterday said that it had breached its legal duty to protect animals from unnecessary suffering during experiments at one of its laboratories.

An internal inquiry, accepted by the council, also attacked the Home Office for allowing the council to operate outside the law.

The experiments were conducted last year by Professor Wilhelm Feldberg at the National Institute for Medical Research, Mill Hill, north London, which is funded by the council. Their colleague prompted anger that set out as designed to prevent suffering had not always been observed but

Prof Wilhelm Feldberg ... caused 'needless suffering'

Professor Feldberg and John Stean, his assistant, lost their licences to experiment after the publicity. The inquiry found the rabbits endured unnecessary suffering and "provided for no discernible benefit to man".

The Heads of Research Councils can

sugar levels that he thought might be related to diabetes.

The inquiry report said that it was hard to understand why the

Lab cruelty leads to tighter checks

HENICK researchers used animals by a lion a leading scientist who caused unnecessary suffering.

The inquiry found that animals in an experiment in his research at a laboratory was "unnecessary suffering" and "provided for no discernible benefit to man".

Advocates for the Scottish group that one opinion happen at a laboratory animal work and Scottish group that investigation was over followed up in any one operation must.

The most failure

A BEAUTIFUL SPY EXPOSED LAB HORROR

STAR EXCLUSIVE: How Melody hoodwinked

Scientist, 90, may be jailed

by GRAHAM KEELEY

REVELATIONS of animal abuse by an internationally renowned Mill Hill scientist will affect the treatment of animals used for medical research throughout the country.

As a report by the Medical Research Council said, the ninety-year-old Professor Wilhelm Feldberg experiments at the National Institute for Medical Research (NIMR), at the Kidneyes, called for

rabbits and one in experiments and blood sugar levels relating to diabetes.

A notice has been to undergrowth experiments.

Profesor McDonald and Max Mannison from the Cruelty to Animals act...

Investigations Ltd...

measuring...

The report said the animals suffered mounting pain through the noise experiments.

Professor Feldberg, at Vasto Lane, and wattles in the centre for trial of state, as an inmate enmeshed, suffered losing comfort and moved indoors.

Dossier reveals 'sad drama' of professor's experiments

By ROBBIE DINWOODIE

Grisly dossier reveals failure of research code

By ROBBIE DINWOODIE

THE CRY is that, high and curiously human Screaming out and out to a sympathetic table, the creature strives on, bucks and thrashes furiously, as two experts who in what time it takes the process of welding surgical stitches means engaging in another human we have don't think we're going to get away with it a Prof... one saw

He a servant As so often happens Professor Wilhelm Feldberg and his assistant, animal technician John Stean, dragged in the anaesthetic level right so that the...

As part of the investigation Les Ward was introduced undercover to Stean and Professor Feldberg at the laboratory last month.

NEWS

Animal rights video traps professor who made rabbits suffer

By Roger Highfield, Science Editor

AN 89-YEAR-OLD professor...

- 'A similar submission from a less distinguished applicant *would have been rejected peremptorily.*'

Director, NIMR

- 'Provided facilities for the Professor to continue working for a further five months. *This was not justified and failed to take into account the Professor's capabilities, the almost certain lack of benefit to be derived from the extension, and the sacrifice of a number of animals.*'
- 'The unauthorised experiments carried out by Professor Feldberg...involved the Director in *a breach of his certificate obligations.*'

The Home Office

- 'The Home Secretary failed to weigh adequately the likely benefit of the research against the likely adverse effects on the animals involved... If he had done so, it is reasonably certain that the amendment to the project licence which allowed the heating of animals' abdomen [sic] would not have been granted.'
- 'The Home Office Inspectors failed to comply with their statutory duties when they did not act as promptly and effectively as they should have done when they were becoming increasingly aware of difficulties involving Professor Feldberg. *The publicity forced them to take the action which they should have taken much earlier.*'

The Named Veterinary Surgeon

- 'The contractual arrangements for the named veterinary surgeon provided a number of hours of availability *which was seriously inadequate.*'

THE REPORT ITSELF included several interesting statements:

- 'The named veterinary surgeon described the position as one of responsibility without power.' (p 29)
- 'The Inspectors told us that they *did not see their role as being involved in uncovering improper laboratory procedures.*' (p 36) [Later, the Home Office stated that 'under this Act this is the primary responsibility of personal licensees who have a duty under the law for the care of their animals. It would be wrong to dilute this in any way.'][20]
- 'It has been suggested that Professor Feldberg, as he himself said on the video, never read the scientific papers of others. We do not take this remark too seriously. He demonstrated a puckish sense of humour tinged with playful bravado and is quite likely to have struck something of a posture.' (p 17)
- Although the Home Office had renewed Feldberg's project licence in July 1989 and amended it on 19 September 1989 to cover the heating of animals' abdomens, the project never actually received MRC approval.
- 'We find it difficult to understand, in these circumstances, how the Home Secretary could have met the requirements of Section 5 (4) when he granted this project licence and its amendment. He is required to weigh the benefit likely to accrue—in our view, negligible—against the likely adverse effects on the animals concerned. Those effects—certain rather than likely—were extremely adverse. The animals died.' (p 21)

FOLLOWING THE PRESS briefing on the Report on 4 February 1991, there were extensive articles in newspapers, magazines and medical and scientific journals in Britain and abroad. The article in *The Times*[21] carried the headline 'Top scientist is criticised for cruelty to animals' while that in *The Daily Telegraph*[22] ran 'Animal rights video traps professor who made rabbits suffer'.

Advocates for Animals[23] provided detailed comments on the MRC Inquiry Report. They were as follows:

1. The Inquiry has underestimated the amount of animal suffering.

2. The Inquiry's view on the use of Sagatal for anaesthetising rabbits is unacceptable. The Home Office should not have approved its use by Professor Feldberg.

3. Professor Wilhelm Feldberg, CBE, FRS, by carrying out unauthorised experiments has breached the Animal (Scientific Procedures) Act 1986. The Home Secretary should submit the papers on the case to the Director of Public Prosecutions *for consideration of a prosecution or give his reasons for not so doing.*

4. John Stean was possibly the Deputy Project Licence Holder [this later proved to be the case—JR]. If proved to be the case, he has breached the Animals (Scientific Procedures) Act 1986 by carrying out unauthorised experiments. The Home Secretary should submit the papers on the case to the Director of Public Prosecutions *for consideration of a prosecution, or give his reasons for not doing so.*

5. The MRC were at fault in deferring Professor Feldberg's grant application and this deferment took no account of the sacrifice of animal life which followed.

6. The holder of the Certificate of Designation, Dr Skehel, has failed in his statutory duties under the 1986 Act and *should be severely reprimanded.*

7. The named day-to-day care person has failed in his duties under the 1986 Act and *should be reprimanded.*

8. The named veterinary surgeon has failed in her duties under the 1986 Act and *should be reprimanded.*

9. The Home Secretary failed to weigh adequately the likely benefit of the research against the likely adverse effects on the animals involved and the amended project licence should not have been granted.

10. The Home Office Inspectors failed in their statutory duties under the 1986 Act and *should be severely reprimanded.*
11. The situation which developed at the NIMR is a matter of grave concern and should never have been allowed to happen.

IT IS INTERESTING to note that, contrary to previous practice, the page detailing reprimands and prosecutions was omitted from the Home Office Statistics for 1990,[24] although it did appear for the first time, and rather unexpectedly, in the Animal Procedures Committee Annual Report, 1990.

We are also informed in the Animal Procedures Committee Annual Report for 1990 that *'the licensing system under the Act is based on a system of trust'* and that *'some even serious infringements, like negligently causing excessive pain, do not actually constitute criminal offences under the Act.'*

PREDICTABLY, SOME ANIMAL research supporters have tried to discredit the Feldberg video. One has even claimed that it has been altered by having the sound-track of a screaming rabbit added to it. This claim is, of course, completely untrue. It does however show how reluctant they are to admit the truth, even when it is supported by accurate, timed and dated video-taped evidence. This same evidence was of course accepted by both the Home Office and the MRC Inquiry—which, when all is said and done, is all that really mattered.

CHAPTER SEVEN

In the End...

Jill Russell

IT IS IRONIC that this investigation began because of Feldberg's experiments on conscious animals, yet his licence was revoked under the 1986 Act for experiments on what should have been fully anaesthetised animals.

Although by 1990 Feldberg was no longer licensed to continue his previous conscious animal brain research, similar research continues in Britain today. It is licensed by the Home Office, often paid for by the taxpayer, and has apparently even been undertaken by some members of the Animals Procedures Committee[25] (which is the government's advisory body on animal experimentation).

Politicians also receive advice from the Research Defence Society, which exists principally to defend animal research. This organisation reports to the members of both houses of parliament to keep them informed about the use of animals in research, and provides information to answer constituents' queries and letters on the subject.

It is therefore no great surprise that the Minister of State at the Home Office has written that she does not accept the need for an increase in the number of Home Office inspectors[26].

Yet in February 1991 there were only 20 inspectors for over 18,000 licensees who had performed almost 3.25 million procedures on living animals in Britain during the previous year.

Following the MRC Inquiry, *there have been no reprimands* and the Home Secretary[27] has announced that there will be *no prosecutions in this case.*

The MRC Secretary, Dr Dai Rees, who in 1993 received a knighthood, said that there would be no MRC disciplinary action.[28] '*We don't see any point in slapping wrists.*'

This investigation has demonstrated that the 1986 Act failed to ensure the humane treatment of animals by research scientists and that the Act can be breached many times, by many people, in many ways, without prosecution or reprimand.

It also demonstrates the exceptional power of the academic and scientific hierarchy. Such hierarchies exist in all walks of life, but where there is suffering as a result of people being afraid to speak out, it is nothing less than tyranny.

Despite Advocates for Animals' comments and recommendations following the MRC Inquiry, the exposé resulted in only one change to the regulations: the Home Office announced publicly in September 1991 that from April 1992 there would be an upper age limit of 70 for project licence holders (except in exceptional circumstances), and annual reviews for personal licensees over that age. Despite this, in August 1992 there were still forty personal licensees aged 70 or over.

However, in October 1992, in a letter from the Home Office to my MP, it was stated that 'information about the number of project licence holders over the age of 70 is not held centrally... While it would be possible to collate this information I believe it would be an unacceptable cost in resources and I therefore regret that I cannot supply the information.'

The impact of this change in the regulations is therefore unknown but, however small it is, we must hope that it will save animals' lives and will help to prevent animal suffering.

Looking to the future, there is no doubt that this and other undercover investigations have raised public awareness of what is going on behind the closed doors of vivisection laboratories.

Most medical doctors have had little or no idea of what is going on in animal research laboratories in their name. However, recent years have seen the formation of British, European and other groups of medical doctors who oppose animal experiments entirely on scientific grounds. With the amassing of video-taped evidence such as this, both they, with their medical knowledge, and informed patients are becoming increasingly tired of being used as scapegoats for such experiments.

This and other investigations have also helped to open up the whole debate on animal experimentation. Lord Houghton of Sowerby commented as follows regarding the APC:

> Perhaps an independent viewpoint on what that body does would be beneficial, otherwise we are in for more undercover work. After all, such undercover work apparently plays an important part in the disturbance that exists in the public's mind as to the use of animals without their knowledge. The trouble in the Quorn Hunt was made known through undercover work. Feldberg's work was made known through undercover work. There are other undercover jobs in progress now because people are determined to find out the truth.[29]

These exposés have also made scientists more aware of the problems of using animals in research. Feldberg's experiments have been described by one scientist as 'astonishing and barbaric'.[30]

New Scientist recently published an eight-part series of articles[31] on the problems of vivisection, and the following quotations from animal research workers who were interviewed illustrate very clearly the new awareness:

- 'Few scientists have much, if any, training in animal husbandry or behaviour, and most are not well equipped to assess if an animal is suffering: "Ninety-nine per cent of scientists don't know anything about whether an animal is feeling pain or not." '
- 'We don't actually have a way of measuring pain.'
- 'A third researcher in the group emphasised the lack of knowledge of the inspectors, explaining that they had to train one about sheep husbandry.'

- 'Complaining that the inspectors had had little opportunity to see what they were doing, one scientist explained that his licence covered procedures that he had never done before, yet he could "wade in with a hangover on a Monday morning" and carry them out.'
- 'Another commented, "...I don't think that modifying the law would get rid of those people [doing bad experiments]." '
- 'One young researcher said: "There's no measure of competence really... it's all done on trust. They [the Home Office] trust the people who've had a licence for 20 years to know what they're doing... For a year I had to be supervised, then I'm just sort of deemed to be competent." '

Three further excerpts from the same *New Scientist* article are particularly appropriate in the light of Feldberg's previous work on conscious cats:

- 'One researcher...felt unhappy about withdrawing fluid from the brain... It would, he said, give him "the creeps" and make him "cringe"...'
- 'One said, for example, that under the old Act people used to "do very cruel things..." '
- 'Another was repelled by "any drugs that prevent an animal from physically responding to whatever is done with it, yet leave it conscious of its environment—they are horror stories." '

PROFESSOR FELDBERG'S EXPERIMENTS were defended by the Home Office and the scientific establishment right up until the very last moment when the video-taped evidence was produced, whereupon hands were held up in horror as if Feldberg had been some unknown little man working in secret in a small back street laboratory in a remote part of the country.

The fact is that the videotaped experiments took place in one of the most prestigious British research institutes. They were carried out by one of Britain's most eminent scientists under what have been stated by the Home Office[32] to be the most rigorous laboratory animal welfare laws in the world.

This investigation demonstrates without doubt the power of the video-recorder. Whereas previous lobbying over many years had proved fruitless, the work of Feldberg and Stean was stopped dead within twenty-four hours of the video-taped evidence being made public.

The personal and project licences of the two vivisectors were revoked. In one case, presumably Feldberg, the licence was 'suspended immediately in the interests of animal welfare'.

It is a good confidence booster for the animal rights movement to demonstrate the successes that can be achieved through totally lawful investigations. Two years later, the investigation was still being endorsed by *The Independent*[33] as an example of non-violent but effective campaigning. Photographs and video clips from the exposé are still being used by the media to illustrate the subject of vivisection.

Animal welfarists who feel daunted by the extent of animal cruelty, but who would like to do something about it, must never feel beaten or alone. They must never give up. They should realise that this exposé was—as can be gathered—totally unplanned. But it was very soon realised that what was happening in the laboratory was confirming all our suspicions about animal experiments, and really did have to be exposed. It was very fortunate that Mike Huskisson came on the scene when he did, for without his video-recorded evidence no-one would have been believed and nothing would have been achieved.

Long after we have all gone, the images captured by camera and on video-tape will endure and those who so arrogantly assert that the 1986 Act ensures that all is well in animal research laboratories will always be haunted by the brutal truth revealed in this investigation.

This is only the beginning. Lord Houghton is quite right. There are other undercover investigations in progress now and there will be more and more exposés until the tyranny of animal experiments and animal abuse is stopped.

Afterword

Mike Huskisson

WE LIVE IN a cruel world. Cruelty is rampant and that cruelty is entirely from the hand of man. It is cruelty inflicted on our own species and cruelty inflicted on those other species that share this planet with us.

Those of us who seek to battle against this have a problem: namely, that we live in a high-tech world. A world in which haunting images of suffering and cruelty are beamed into the homes of people day after day after day. Television is full of the sights of cruelty, the radio is full of the sounds, and the papers are full of the images. Is it any wonder that the public are at times apathetic? Is it any wonder that people at times feel helpless?

Of course most of the suffering we see concerns our own species and that commands the greatest attention. There are images of suffering from starvation, images of pain as the result of wars, images of anguish that results from oppression and ignorance. It seems to be cruelty without end.

When we ask the public to extend their circle of compassion from their own species to their fellow creatures we need to provide good evidence for them to do so.

Of course, in an ideal world, we should be able to expect compassion from our fellow citizens towards other creatures as a right, but the world is by no means ideal. Those who take profit or pleasure from mistreating animals have no intention of allowing the question to be resolved as a moral issue. To protect their interest, they seek to cloud the debate with a profusion of lies, deceit and half-truths.

We are told that without factory farming the world would starve, that without vivisection the world would succumb to sickness and disease, that without bloodsports a nation would lose its moral fibre and the countryside would be knee deep in pests.

Such are the utterings of the ignorant, but they cannot be exposed as such by words alone. We need to produce hard evidence to sustain our views. Of the three main animal welfare issues—vivisection, factory farming and bloodsports—it is in the area of vivisection that it is hardest to come up with the evidence. This is because it takes place behind doors that are closed by tradition. Nowadays they are also locked, bolted, have security cameras and are patrolled by security guards!

Scientists usually publish a précis of the research they do. Indeed it is the aspiration to publish that mainly motivates their research in the first place. From these reports, despite being couched in euphemisms, we can glean an insight into the suffering entailed. But this is rarely enough to win the debate to end such cruelty in the public forum. To do that we need to gain entry ourselves with the means to record all that really happens.

In the seventies the concept arose of forcing an entry into laboratories to rescue animals, destroy equipment and gather evidence. This achieved some success. Some animals were saved, albeit only a tiny fraction of those that suffered. However, the public saw a lot more of what was really meant by the word vivisection.

The cost to the multinationals who undertake research in the UK rose dramatically. Hundreds of thousands of pounds were spent on providing security for laboratories. The equipment that was smashed undoubtedly set the research back, but it was usually completed eventually. The laboratories frequently ended up with bright shiny new equipment thanks to insurance claims, though the premiums subsequently rose dramatically.

As such attacks progressed through the eighties, it looked for a time as if vivisection might be driven out of this country by such actions.

There are plenty of nearby countries where animal welfare is virtually unheard of, let alone the concept of animal rights. It would be easy and cost-effective in the face of such attacks for a multinational to move their whole operation abroad.

Not surprisingly, the establishment struck back against the pro-animal sector. In a series of show trials the leaders were imprisoned. The movement was infiltrated and neutered. A dirty tricks department really went to town with a series of bizarre incidents in which animal rights activists supposedly sought to attack and injure members of the public. The direct action wing of the movement was fairly effectively suppressed by the state.

When considering aggression and violence as a feature in this debate we must never forget the Greenpeace photographer who was killed by state sponsored terrorism when his ship was blown up in New Zealand.

Elements within the animal welfare movement then sought to advance their campaigns by developing tactics of lawful investigation. Entry would be gained to laboratories by using brain rather than brawn. Our people would make friendly contact to talk their way in. Our people would apply for jobs, not just in the obvious role of animal technicians, but also as cleaners, secretaries, drivers, even security men! Any way to gain access.

The effectiveness of this style of campaigning had already been demonstrated by the media years before. Who can forget the brilliant exposé of the smoking beagles at ICI, achieved by a reporter for *The People* working under cover? But the animal welfare movement was slow to learn this lesson. For a considerable time the boot in the door tactic proved more attractive than the patience required for lengthy undercover work.

However, undercover work was to have its day and Melody was one of the first to practise it effectively and expose the academic side of the animal research business. Many were aware from books and leaflets of Feldberg's experiments on conscious cats. Many read and were shocked. But it was Melody who set about doing something about it. She then showed the determination and perseverance to see the matter through.

Much time was to elapse from her initial entry to the laboratory until she was put in touch with my organisation, the Animal Cruelty Investigation Group, but those dark days of frustrating delays only enhanced her determination to see the research exposed. From our very first meeting in December 1989 the days of Feldberg's research were numbered.

Although only formally in existence for a matter of months at the time, the ACIG was already well experienced in this kind of work. We were and are supported by a committed, dedicated and generous group of people and accordingly were able to purchase all the expensive photographic equipment needed to do the job.

We also found, in Advocates for Animals, a major animal rights group with the necessary professional expertise to publicise the story, and convey it to the government in the most effective manner. As a result, less than twenty-four hours after 'going public', Feldberg and Stean lost their licences to experiment on animals. This was a copybook operation for the ACIG and one in which we are proud and pleased to have taken part.

We believe that the essential element for ending vivisection, factory farming and blood sports is first to expose exactly what is going on. The public cannot be expected to offer opinions on the rights or wrongs of these issues when they are ill-informed. Our opponents can only survive if the ignorance is maintained.

Our job is to cut through the secrecy and ignorance to reveal the truth. That we will do and furthermore we will do it lawfully. If anyone is to encounter legal difficulties at the hands of the authorities it will be our opponents. The MRC Report reveals that Feldberg could have been charged with infringing the 1986 Act. It is believed that only his advanced age saved him from this fate. The next scientists we expose may well not be so lucky.

Finally, it is pleasing to note a boom in this style of video campaign work. In 1991 the National Anti-Vivisection Society produced 'Vivisection in Britain' describing conditions at SmithKline Beecham Pharmaceutical Laboratories and at St Bartholomew's Medical School. Even more recently the British

Union for the Abolition of Vivisection exposed the primate trade through their remarkable 'Paradise Lost' project. This entailed many months of, at times, very dangerous undercover work. Other similar work is in the pipeline.

This is the way forward for our movement. We have the people, we have the determination, the equipment is available and with the help of those who read this we can have the necessary finance.

Sooner or later the cruelty of vivisection will end. It is only a question of which generation will do the job, and how many animals will suffer and die in the meantime. Are we going to set to and do the job here and now—or are we going to leave the task to our children? We are not here to protest at cruelty, we are here to end it.

Publisher's note: Professor Feldberg died in November 1993 while this book was in production.

References

1. People for the Ethical Treatment of Animals. *Unnecessary Fuss.* Washington DC, PETA, 1984.
2. Ruesch, H. *Slaughter of the Innocent.* New York, CIVITAS Publication1983, p103.
3. Feldberg, W.S., Pyke, D.A., Stubbs W.A. *The Lancet,* 1985; i: 1263.
4. Feldberg, W.S. *Fifty Years On: Looking back on some Developments in Neurohumoral Physiology.* Liverpool, Liverpool University Press 1982, p1.
5. Feldberg W., Sherwood S.L. 'Injections of drugs into the lateral ventricle of the cat', in *J Physiol* 1954; 123: 148.
6. Bergmann F., Feldberg W. 'Effects of propylbenzilylcholine mustard on injection into the liquor space of cats', in *Brit J Pharmacol* 1978; 63: 3.
7. Feldberg W., Fleischhauer K. 'A new experimental approach to the physiology and pharmacology of the brain', in *Brit Med Bull* 1965; 21(1): 36.
8. RSPCA. *Pain and Suffering in Experimental Animals in the United Kingdom.* Horsham, RSPCA, 1983.
9. Feldberg, W.S. *Fifty Years On: Looking back on some Developments in Neurohumoral Physiology.* Liverpool, Liverpool University Press 1982, p5.
10. Schilf, E., Feldberg, W.S. 'Beitrag zur Kenntnis der Hautdruseninnervation des Frosches', in *Pfluger's Archiv für die gesamte Physiologie* 1923; 200: 235.
11. Feldberg, W.S. *Fifty Years On: Looking back on some Developments in Neurohumoral Physiology.* Liverpool, Liverpool University Press 1982, p80.
12. Part of this film is included in 'Exposed', a video published by Advocates for Animals, 1991.
13. Feldberg, W.S. *Fifty Years On: Looking back on some Developments in Neurohumoral Physiology.* Liverpool, Liverpool University Press 1982, p42.
14. Medical Research Council: Inquiry into the operation of the Animals (Scientific Procedures) Act 1986 and the administrative procedures within the MRC in relation to experiments carried out by Professor W.S. Feldberg. Report of the Inquiry, 1991.
15. *The Independent,* 9th May, 1990.
16. *The Glasgow Herald,* 9th May, 1990.
17. *Edgware and Mill Hill Times,* 10th May, 1990.
18. Douglas, W.W. and others. *Nature* 1990; 345: 657.

19. *The Times*, 5 February 1991.
20. Rumbold, A. Personal communication, 10 April 1991.
21. *The Times*, 5 February 1991.
22. *The Daily Telegraph*, 5 February 1991.
23. Advocates for Animals. *Comments on the Report of the MRC Inquiry into the Operation of the Animals (Scientific Procedures) Act 1986 and the Administrative Procedures within the MRC in Relation to Experiments Carried out by Professor W S Feldberg.* 29 April, 1991.
24. Home Office. *Statistics of Scientific Procedures on Living Animals in Great Britain 1990.*
25. *Liberator*, Spring 1991.
26. Rumbold, A. Personal communication, 14 November 1991.
27. *Parliamentary Review*, 13 December 1991.
28. *Nature,* 1991; 349: 446.
29. *Hansard*, 27 November 1991.
30. *Scotland on Sunday*, 4 August 1991.
31. Michael, M., Birke, L. 'The Researchers' Dilemma', in *New Scientist*, 4 April 1992, pp25-32.
32. Rumbold, A. Personal communication, 20 February 1990.
33. Editorial in *The Independent*, 14 November 1991.

For more information about vivisection and how you can help to end it, please contact:

Advocates for Animals
10 Queensferry Street, Edinburgh EH2 4PG.
☎ 031 225 6039.

Animal Aid
7 Castle Street, Tonbridge, Kent TN9 1BH.
☎ 0732 264546.

Animal Concern
62 Old Dumbarton Road, Glasgow G3 8RE.
☎ 041 334 6014.

Animal Cruelty Investigation Group
PO Box 8, Halesworth, Suffolk IP19 0JL.

British Anti-Vivisection Association (BAVA)
PO Box 82, Kingswood, Bristol BS15 1YF.

British Union for the Abolition of Vivisection (BUAV),
16a Crane Grove, London N7 8LB.
☎ 071 700 4888.

Disabled Against Animal Research and Exploitation (DAARE)
PO Box 8, Daventry, Northants NN11 4RQ.

Doctors in Britain Against Animal Experiments (DBAE),
PO Box 302, London N8 9HD.

European Medical Journal
Dr Vernon Coleman, Lynmouth, Devon EX35 6EE.

National Anti-Vivisection Society (NAVS)
Ravenside, 261 Goldhawk Road, London W12 9PE.
☎ 081 846 9777.

Plan 2000 (to stop vivisection by 2000AD)
234 Summergangs Road, Hull HU8 8LL.